Chanakya *in the* Classroom

TIMELESS WISDOM FOR STUDENTS

Chanakya *in the* Classroom

TIMELESS WISDOM FOR STUDENTS

MAHESH DUTT SHARMA

PRABHAT
PRAKASHAN

Published by
PRABHAT PRAKASHAN PVT. LTD.
4/19 Asaf Ali Road,
New Delhi-110 002 (INDIA)
e-mail: prabhatbooks@gmail.com

ISBN 978-93-5521-790-5
CHANAKYA IN THE CLASSROOM: TIMELESS WISDOM FOR STUDENTS
by Mahesh Dutt Sharma

Edition
First, 2023

Price
₹ 250 (Rupees Two Hundred Fifty Only)

Printed at
Sanjay Printers, Sahibabad

Author's Note

Along with being a diplomat, the great economist Acharya Chanakya was also a skilled teacher. He guided Chandragupta from mediocrity to excellence with his instructions in education and helped him gain the highest seat of power. Chanakya has also articulated his personal lofty and practical educational philosophy for students in his work on ethics—*Chanakya Neeti*. By practising his educational philosophy, even an ordinary student can move forward on the path of extraordinary progress.

Acharya Chanakya has also mentioned student life as an important stage in education. He has chronicled its essence in one single verse. The verse of Acharya Chanakya is as follows:

Kamkrodhau tatha lobham swayu shrungarkauturake

Atinidratiseve ch vidyarthi mhasht varjyet

That is to say, sex, anger, greed, gustation, intercourse (Rati), amusement (entertainment), hypersomnia and excess service—those who aspire for learning should give up these eight things.

With the above verse, Acharya Chanakya has given a message to the students which can lead them to definite success. This book presents a detailed description of Acharya Chanakya's educational philosophy so that students can experience all round development by understanding his educational messages in detail.

This is a readable, inspiring and collectible book.

Author's Note

Contents

1 Acharya Chanakya's Educational Message

"Sex, anger, greed, gustation, intercourse (Rati), amusement (entertainment), hypersomnia and excess service – those who aspire for learning should give up these eight things."

–Chanakya

We are always learning in life, and from that standpoint, we are all students. Only education gives the right direction to a person's life. Only good education can help make a good future. For this reason, special care should be taken by the students during their student life. During that period, if a student deviates from the path, then his whole life can be badly affected.

Education is very important for giving the right direction to life; only good education can create a good future. If a student deviates from his path during his student life, his entire life can be badly affected. So, Acharya Chanakya has shared many secrets of success for the students. Chanakya believes that it is very important to pay attention to some things while studying. Chanakya has spoken of a few such things from which it is better for the students to stay away.

According to Acharya Chanakya, to achieve success in life, it is very important for a person to follow certain rules. People cannot taste success if they ignore these rules. So, in order to achieve one's goals in life, some special rules have been prescribed for the students in *Chanakya Neeti*.

Acharya Chanakya says that in order to receive education, it is very important for both mind and brain to be calm. An angry mind cannot receive the education properly. With a restless mind, the student only listens to the knowledge being imparted; he is unable to grasp it and follow it.

In fact, some very useful tips are included in the Acharya Chanakya's *Chanakya Neeti*. By following these tenets, any student can be successful in getting education in the best and correct way and can become capable of reaching his goal, every target in his life.

We will discuss these tenets further in detail so that you can understand them better and adopt them and bring about a major change in your life. Chanakya has presented the knowledge accumulated from his experiences to people of all ages and classes.

'Learning' or 'gaining knowledge' is an activity that continues throughout life. Throughout our life, we keep learning something new; sometimes circumstances teach us something, at other times, we learn for self-improvement. But whenever education is mentioned, a student's image comes to the mind.

Of all the phases of life, student life is probably the most important phase because if it is handled with patience, then life will be successful, otherwise even a small mistake can destroy the whole future. Therefore, it is the responsibility of both teachers and parents to give the child a good education.

The great diplomat and economist Acharya Chanakya has also mentioned student life as an important stage in education. He has chronicled its essence in one single verse. The verse of Acharya Chanakya is as follows –

Kamkrodhau tatha lobham swayu shrungarkauturake

Atinidratiseve ch vidyarthi mhasht varjyet

That is to say, sex, anger, greed, gustation, intercourse (Rati), amusement (entertainment), hypersomnia and excess service – those who aspire for learning should give up these eight things.

With the above verse, Acharya Chanakya has given a message to the students which can lead them to definite success. So, let us understand these life messages of Acharya Chanakya's in detail.

❑

2 Guarding Against Sexual Urge

"Before beginning any task, ask yourself three questions – Why am I doing this, what will be its consequences and will I succeed? It is advisable to proceed only if you get satisfactory answers to these questions after pondering over them deeply".

–Chanakya

The word sex commonly implies the relationship between a man and a woman. Students who want to study or achieve their goals do not fall into this kind of bad company. The person whose mind is occupied with the thoughts of sex continues to be restless all the time. Such a person adopts any means, right or wrong, to fulfill his desires.

If a student gets caught in the sexual feelings, then he can never achieve success. He puts his entire life at stake for the momentary pleasure. His entire attention is focused only towards the fulfillment of his sexual desires and he drifts away from studies. Hence, students should avoid such feelings.

Even if the students obsessed with the sexual feelings try to focus on their studies, the thoughts raging through their minds destroy their concentration. Such students have to work very hard to achieve success because their mind always wanders due to the thoughts of sexual feelings. Hence, it is best for students to stay away from sexual acts.

Sexual feeling is the greatest weakness of human mind. Though a person wants to get rid of sexual feelings and live a life of celibacy, the storms of emotion arise in his mind again and again and make him distraught. The inner feelings keep on stirring and rousing and captivating the mind.

Measures to Stop the Sexual Feelings from Arousing

Do not encourage sexual feelings: Do not desire lustful things. Avoid watching pornography, provocative and erotic things. Learn to control the mind regarding these things. Meditate in the morning and evening. This will calm your mind and increase concentration, with which you can overcome your bad feelings. By fighting the body, by suppressing the body, by whipping the body, by laying the body on thorns, by sitting under the sun, or by laying the body on ice – no matter how much one tortures the body, no matter how much one troubles the body, one cannot bring the body under control. Troubling the body and torturing the body – this is also being done by the body. The body can never be controlled like this. Yes, it can become weak, it can become frail, and it can become feeble. And weakness creates the deception that the body has been brought under control.

Understand your feelings: Sexual feelings are mentioned as being natural in all the religious texts of the world, but after a certain age. So, do not feel ashamed of yourself if you have sexual feelings. Understand these feelings and try to stop them because during student life, it is necessary to suppress and restrain these emotions.

Divert your attention: When you get such thoughts and cannot think of any solution, then focus your attention somewhere else, like reading an interesting book, in sports, etc. In this way, you will slowly get rid of that thought.

Make a list and stay away from those things: Make a list of those activities or things that arouse sexual feelings in you, such as pornography or obscene literature, or write down or memorize whatever other emotions that take you towards sexual feelings and pledge not to go near those things at all.

Make yourself busy: This is an effective way. If you keep yourself completely busy in some work, then you will not have the opportunity to have sensual thoughts in your mind. For this, you can join any social work group where you can also do social service during your spare time and also avoid having sensual thoughts. No one can conquer the body by fighting the body. No one can control the mind by fighting the mind. You can overpower something only when you experience an element that is beyond it. Otherwise, it is not possible to conquer it.

When a youth gets entangled in such things, he is not able to pay attention to his studies and health. He becomes sluggish due to the sensual thoughts whereas it is his age of learning and staying active. Therefore, students should avoid these types of thoughts.

❑

3 Anger is Enemy

"One who has no knowledge, no tenacity, no charity and no religion, he roams like the deer in the form of a burdensome human in this land of death. In fact, such a person's life is meaningless. He is of no use to the society."

–Chanakya

Acharya Chanakya says that anger makes a man blind, he cannot differentiate between right and wrong, which only causes him harm; he drifts apart from his well-wishers, loved ones, family, and even himself. Due to anger, the person gets aggravated at small things and does something for which he has to repent later.

Anger and ego have only destroyed people like Ravana and Kansa. The mind of an angry person is never calm. While receiving education with a disturbed mind, the person only listens to the knowledge, he never understands it nor can he follow it.

Therefore, in order to receive education, it is very important for a person to control his anger.

Resolving Anger Issues

Anger is a sign of abnormal behaviour. It is a process through which human development and adaptation is blocked. Anger in itself is not a bad thing, but problems arise when it is not handled properly. It is foolish to show impatience, nervousness again and again; it shows lack of control, understanding and sensitivity. Anger involves both emotional and physical changes. When a person is angry or nervous, a type of hormone called 'adrenal' comes out of living cells. A large amount of energy is released from your body when chemicals like 'adrenaline' are released. Even after the cause of anger is resolved, you may have to deal with its physical effects so that you can drain the excess energy or destroy it. You can take it out on another person, your partner, or you can erase it by kicking or hitting the wall.

Anger and annoyance are fundamental feelings that are easily expressed when people feel that they have not been treated properly. When something is not done the way they want it to be done and when they feel hurt or humiliated, they are unable to control their behaviour and often become angry at the mistakes of others. Anger and annoyance both have a close relationship and these feelings are expressed much more among relatives and close associates. For example, annoyance can turn into anger when someone does not understand what has just been said. One gets annoyed with the questions that are asked frequently. Relatives or friends may feel that there is no solution to their constant harassment. People get angry and they can also beat up others and later feel very ashamed.

People are convinced that their reaction is natural since this is a common reaction seen in most people and can be justified in a rational way. But rational thinking cannot explain why people become so angry and impatient when some work gets spoiled or the situation does not remain favourable. It is only a presumption that it is a rational behaviour and that it can be forgiven and justified provided it is clear as to why the person feels that he has been treated unfairly.

There would be no point in stating that when someone hurts them, they react with aggression and anger. The reason for the impulsive aggressive reaction arising from anger and irritation is that the mental sphere has an unrestrained and intense reason which controls people's behaviour when their ego and self-esteem are hurt for some reason. If that was not the case, there would not have been that kind of angry response. The person is only restless and unhappy, and not angry. Anger and furious reactions are ludicrous and absurd, because people should make a sensible effort to understand what is causing their suffering without getting angry. First of all, it is important to know what positive and negative feelings you get from anger. It is necessary to identify both emotions – positive and negative – related to the situation to explore other measures and to focus on positive emotions.

Different people have different feelings. For this reason, the situations will also be different. However, there are some tips that may prove useful for many of them, such as –

- Remember that you are a human being and it is desirable to remain a human being. People will often forget the incident caused by your uncontrolled behaviour. However, it is worth knowing how to control your emotions and irritation. If it has become a recurring problem, then it is better to consult someone or take advice about your anger.
- You do not have to be embarrassed about your feelings and behaviour. But try to understand why you get livid, why you become angry so that you can deal with these situations.
- Take the time to laugh. This will help you deal with the difficult situation and see the events in the right perspective.
- It is advisable to seek the help of your family, friends, relatives and corresponding organizations so that you do not break down.
- Trying a non-contacting competitive sport.
- Contemplating or learning to relax.
- Shouting alone in a quiet place.

- Running.
- Hitting a pillow.

If all these measures do not improve your condition, then sit down properly and try to understand what exactly makes you angry and upset. It will often involve a person or people. Therefore, perhaps it is advisable to approach the same people first to solve the problem. The important thing is that you remember that you only have to focus on the problem and face the problem and not the person.

Determine what the problem is and what it makes you feel. Again, determine that it is the problem and not the person who forces you to think like that. It is also important to understand each other's view of the situation. Everyone should be able to express their opinion about the problem or whatever they think about it without being interrupted by others. Then determine the points on which you do not agree. Don't argue about those disagreements and differences at that point. Just agree with the disagreements. This is how the problem is determined.

The next step would be to find a suitable solution. Here, you can go to any extent. But then remember, there should be no personal attack. Find as many solutions as you can – possible and impossible, realistic and unrealistic. At such times, it doesn't really matter. And in the end, you have to accept one of the solutions. This is probably the most delicate and essential part of the whole process. The important thing is not to have unrealistic expectations. May be the final solution is not detrimental for either of you. But whatever solution eventually comes up, it will probably be better than anger-related problems. However, if a person is unable to deal with this problem alone or even with the help of others, then it is necessary for him to resort to psychiatric help so that he can learn to control his reactions and overcome the problem.

If you decide to just keep calm, then it will not prove useful in practical life because it is not a question that depends only on your desire and wish. It is already a subject related to the anti-consciousness element, which is deeply entrenched in you and penetrates into your personality and tries to destroy it.

Therefore, you should follow the characters like Sri Ram and Krishna. It is very important for the mind to be calm and single-minded in order to attain knowledge.

❑

4 Rivalry, Not Jealousy

"Learning cannot be acquired from reading books; it is obtained from the close association with the Guru. The scholar who acquires the knowledge from books alone is considered ignoble in the assembly in the same way that a licentious woman is not honoured in the society even when she conceives".

–Chanakya

Acharya Chanakya says that jealousy keeps the person burning inside like fire. The fire of jealousy makes the man angry. He keeps looking for opportunities to put people down. The feeling of jealousy makes the thoughts of a human being cloudy. Wrong thoughts are born in his mind. Wrong thoughts lead man to the wrong path. Remember, jealousy burns you while rivalry elevates you.

Jealousy, anger, greed, pride, etc. are all enemies of the conscience. When a man is jealous of another man's success, he loses his conscience and incites other people against him. When a person is impatient, he gets angry. Losing his balance due to anger, he becomes unscrupulous and harms himself as well as becoming detrimental to others. When a man becomes highly attracted towards something, then greed occupies his mind. He tries to obtain that thing through illegal means. He also adopts violent methods. There is only one thought in his mind that he has to acquire that thing by any means no matter what he has to do for it, and this is the moment when man becomes unwise.

Jealousy is such a dangerous and intoxicating insect that once it bites a human being, he always remains intoxicated by it. But he only gets unhappiness because he gets distressed by seeing other peoples' progress. The other person is happy, so there is jealousy; the other person is beautiful, so there is jealousy; why am I not progressing, the other person is progressing, so there is jealousy. He is friendly with everybody, he behaves nicely with everyone, everybody likes him and not me, so there is jealousy. You should also become that kind of a person so that you would not need to be jealous of anyone.

God has honoured man with the pride of creation. We should not ignore its importance. We should be as creative as possible. Use the creation of God and decorate yourself with your best qualities and create the best things. The lives of the people who make the best of circumstances also become excellent themselves.

God has made man the best among all beings so that he reaches all the heights for which he has taken birth. In a deeper sense, we have remained an unbroken part of this universe since time immemorial. We have been arriving at different times and in different countries. There are signs of this somewhere in all our scriptures. We just should not give up the enthusiasm and keep moving forward towards our goal.

Enthusiasm is that important quality of man that doubles his other qualities such as determination, self-confidence, patience, prudence, etc., due to which that person works without hindrance and succeeds. The work done with lack of enthusiasm is never complete because if the beginning is not proper, then how can the end be good? If a person works with enthusiasm, he does not work only for himself. Rather on seeing him, the enthusiasm of other people also increases because when they see him achieving success by working enthusiastically, they feel that they too can achieve it. They too are filled with enthusiasm by taking inspiration, i.e., seeing the enthusiasm of the person, the people around him are also filled with enthusiasm. But only those who want to achieve success take such inspiration.

On the other hand, unenthusiastic, depressed, frustrated and dejected people are filled with a feeling of worthlessness. They feel that they cannot do anything in life. They are upset due to their small mistakes and always think about them. They want to cry, scream and shout. They often have suicidal thoughts. With the thought of overcoming this sadness, many people resort to addictions. By getting intoxicated, they feel that they can overcome this problem, at least for some time.

Melancholic people do not like radio, TV programmes, children running around and shouting, etc. Laziness overpowers them right from morning. They do not like to leave their bed, shaving daily, bathing, wearing nice clothes, etc. This type of person also does not take interest in any work, sports or recreation. They do not feel hungry and are not interested in delicious and tasty food.

There is no goal in their life. They are only 'letting time pass', i.e., they are just spending life. They lack leadership. They are left behind. They do not understand that they lack faith.

Very few people understand that our bold mistakes become the steps for success. A defeat is not the cause of our failure. Rather the failure to recognize the learning, the advice and the experience that is hidden in the defeat make us fail. We should learn to accept the responsibilities associated with our mistakes and achievements.

Chanakya says that the sculpture is hidden within the stone, there is no need to make it; only the extra stone that is attached to it needs to be separated and then the sculpture will be revealed.

The sculpture is not made, it is just refined, discovered, exposed, revealed.

There is a saying – 'Sleep wiser.', i.e., we must learn something every day. We should not sleep the same way that we had woken up in the morning.

Make a diary. Write in it how you spend your day. By doing this, you will know how much time you have given to non-essential work. Make a daily plan. Make this plan before you go to sleep at night or when you get up in the morning. From this, you will know what you are going to do throughout the day. Then you will continue to do your work according to your plan. If you assess yourself when you are alone, you will definitely be able to identify your shortcomings. Keep in mind that there is nothing bigger in this world than time, which you should spend with full understanding and maturity.

Then after determining a specific direction, build your capabilities. Specific livelihoods require specialized education and training. You will succeed in whatever field you choose provided that you try to be the best in it and leave your personal impression on it. Understand the basics of every task by gaining information. For this, you can opt for a course while being under-training and opt for business during summer. You can learn and understand the economics of work. You can acquire those special abilities with the help of which you will be able to do that work more efficiently.

When a child learns to walk, he falls several times, then gets up and walks again. And thus, he learns to walk because he gains confidence to stand and succeeds.

Rise above the illusory assumptions and know that success is not a result of specific circumstances or attitude. Often it is the result of success-oriented behaviour, in which those characteristics or qualities play a part which one can learn and develop. There is no secret way to achieve success. Rather the path to success is open to anyone who has a goal and who adopts the characteristics commonly seen in all successful people, i.e., their thinking, attitude and behaviour.

Once, a small pencil of Gandhiji's was misplaced. He spent two hours looking for it and was relieved when he found it. He knew that if small things were neglected then the man would develop the same bad habit for bigger things.

Once, the wide road said to the footpath, "I think you are always walking around me". The footpath politely replied, "I don't know why people like to walk on me even though you are there although I am much smaller than you".

Once a person went to the great philosopher Socrates and asked him the secret to be successful in life. The next day, Socrates took the person in the middle of the river. When the water level of the river reached the nose of the person and he found it difficult to breath, he started struggling to breathe. But Socrates still kept his neck submerged under water. In the end, when he felt that the person could die due to lack of breath, he took him out of the river. Socrates told the man that the way he was longing to breathe in the river, we should have the same yearning to get success in our life. This philosophy of Socrates' about success is very important and practical, which also indirectly explains the way of time management.

According to Chanakya, after setting a goal we can focus on it wholeheartedly to achieve it only when we divert our attention from other temptations. When a person makes a particular task his life's goal and performs it, he is completely victorious. By focusing all our powers on a particular purpose, we learn about all the means required to accomplish that task. The errors which obstruct the accomplishment are also gradually realized, which are then easy to overcome. On the contrary, when we do not fully focus on any purpose and continue to disperse our power all over the place, then we do not become aware of the details of that task. We do not even find the right solution for the mistakes or errors of the first task and start the second task. Its results are never satisfactory or appreciable. Bear in mind that the results of half-hearted actions also definitely remain incomplete.

A problem can have many solutions. It is not necessary that the solution chosen by the majority is the right one. You need to understand your problem deeply. For this, brainstorm or analyse your ways or measures in your mind. The newly developed way born from the process of analysis will prove to be helpful in dealing with your problem.

By adding our successes, we build a bridge on which the chariot of our progress then keeps running without stopping. Your concentration helps you in this task. As soon as you are engaged in any work with full focus, half the work is over in the beginning.

It happens when we concentrate. While talking about the principle of concentration, we have to pay attention to two more things. A question arises that when a person has been engaged in the same task with concentration and attachment for years while facing many difficulties and still sees from his own and others' experience that success in this specific work is not possible, then should he take up another task or not? Or should he remain engaged in the same work? If the reason for the success of that work is known after years of experience and then we reach the conclusion that this reason is so strong that it cannot be removed, then it is appropriate to do another work at that time. But it is necessary to think repeatedly and have patience and wait before leaving one task and moving on to another, because it is often seen that by the time the person gets tired of business and starts getting involved in another work out of panic, then he also gets victory in his first task.

There will be times when you will doubt your abilities because many times it will happen that you will try but you will not succeed. Remember that this is a normal thing to happen in this process. Do not get discouraged and do not stop trying just because you have failed a few times in your efforts. Keep a long-term view and think big. Try again. Remember, it is the steps of failures that take a person to the pinnacle of success.

Chanakya asks what kind of occupation or business is there in which there is no obstruction? In any profession, how will one get success without facing the hurdles arising in that profession?

Why is it that some people break down completely or are shattered during difficult situations, while some people not only face those situations very strongly, but they shine even more brightly in adverse circumstances? There is no one in the world who does not have to face unfavourable circumstances in life. But some people have the ability to come out of the most difficult situation successfully by fighting the worst situations.

Anything that makes us get lost in its thoughts can become an asset by which to build our life. We can list those things on the basis of priority by noting them down in a notebook with a pencil. The benefit of writing these desires together will be that we will get a chance to get acquainted with our nature, our expectations, our aspirations and our dreams.

It is difficult to find a person who has never made any mistake. But people who do not repeat a mistake in life after learning a lesson from it are called intelligent. We should correct our mistakes as far as possible. Instead of avoiding the situations, you should face them and then accept the truth while considering God and yourself as witnesses. We should also determine in our mind that from now on we will not make such a mistake. Many times, our relations deteriorate due to financial transactions. In such a situation, we should ask ourselves if money matters more to us or the relationship matters more.

There are also youngsters who are busy in their work or business with enthusiasm and energy. Their determination is unwavering. Continuous effort becomes their second nature. Such young men reach the pinnacle of progress. Analyse great and successful people. The first reason for them to become great will be – self-confidence and only self-confidence. Our history is filled with examples of such great people. They were not liked by the people in their time, but later they were accepted and given highest dignity.

There are a few lucky people who get success in their first attempt. If you ever ask successful people, then you will know how many times they had failed before reaching the destination of success. Therefore, the tendency to think of oneself as the most useless person in the world if one is unsuccessful in an examination is wrong. Many times, the reason for failure is also spending our time and money on a goal which is beyond our capability.

Chanakya tells us to make our goals big. The result will be that you will take a step forward and expand your boundaries towards achieving them. Opportunity is a boon, which does not come again and again in life. Therefore, one should always be ready to welcome the opportunity and take advantage of it with full confidence and faith. Speak according to the occasion. Listen more to the other person, speak less about yourself. A failure is an opportunity when you can start over more wisely.

Actually, successful people win with their constant faith and they also deal with failures with the same faith. Enthusiasm is the jewel of those who want to achieve success. Encouragement acts like an elixir that works wonders for a dying person. While carrying out any work or thinking about any subject, do not let the feeling of indifference and anxiety arise. Think of it as entertainment.

Make up your mind to do something new and take initiative for it. Many people prove their good ideas to be useless and unproductive due to not believing in their abilities. Perform any task sincerely and faithfully and not with a heavy heart. Do not do any work just for the sake of it but to move forward. The crusher bull moves around all day, but remains in the same place.

Thinking rationally about mistakes and accepting them makes a big difference. Emotional reaction to mistakes changes our decisions and creates guilt. The ship is safest when it stays along the coast. But don't you know that it is designed not to remain at the shore but to go in the middle of the sea?

Keep a clear vision about life. Life is like a cycle of ten gears. Many of us have these gears, which we do not use. Whatever work you do, do it with great pleasure. Many times, we make ourselves miserable thinking that we are not doing good work. Whatever you do, do it with all your heart. The more the inner happiness, the more we will be motivated for success.

Praise others with an open mind. Appreciation is a quality that makes everyone your friend. Help others achieve their goals. Give subordinates the right space and authority to perform their roles. Do not be limited to yourself. It is good to be inspired by others, but copying their success does not always work. Accept yourself. Take risks, you will gain experience in the process. Overall, each person is a leader and has the potential to become a leader.

Chanakya advises that instead of copying, one must create. Renounce negative thinking and bring a revolution of positive thoughts in your ideology. Getting continuously educated is better than just being literate. The tendency to make excuses or avoiding makes a man indolent. Solve problems. Do not panic. Failure only paves the way to success. Keep trying continuously.

Highlight the strong side. Know your strong sides and abilities. Psychologists have proven that the boredom, dullness and dissatisfaction in life can be avoided by refining any of our favourite hobbies along with achieving success.

Work hard, but not without a plan. Take one step at a time. When you have taken a step, then prepare. If you want happiness for your whole life, then learn to love your work. Keep doing this work continuously – do extensive study so that the brain can be used. Perform your work as planned, do not waste time. Work in moderation under adverse conditions and face them patiently. This is an important quality of success. Try to remain a normal person by abandoning the distinctiveness.

Always remember these three rules of success - hard work, confidence and self-development. One must wait to be successful. To desire a fruit from a sapling is nothing but foolishness. Cultivate confidence for success. Even if you fail, keep the faith. Understand the importance of time to achieve success. Use it every moment. Do not let the qualities like loneliness, fear, inhibition, emotionality and inferiority get the better of you in order to achieve success. Follow a disciplined way.

Speak thoughtfully as conversation plays an important role in creating and distorting your image. Think that whatever I have is special for me. Develop your ability to make decisions. Develop the nature of learning and experience. Whatever we are, whatever we do, it only happens when we really want to do it.

Start every day with a pleasant, satisfied and happy attitude. You will find that your day will be pleasant and successful. There are many habits that we do not want to give up and then say that they do not leave us. Think about them seriously and ponder. Every time some great man may not be present to teach you, but his words will always be with you.

An opportunity knocks once in every person's life. Try to identify and capture that moment. If you are not able to succeed once, do not waste time by regretting or crying. New opportunities will come your way. All that will be required is your hard work, perseverance and concentration.

❑

5 Greed is Bad

"Those who desire happiness should renounce the hope of learning, a student should give up the hope of happiness. A person desiring happiness cannot hope to learn, a student cannot hope for happiness."

–Chanakya

Greed is an illusion. The student who comes in contact with it cannot remain resolute towards his goal. We have all heard and read that greed is a bad thing. Greedy humans can misuse anyone for their own benefit and can cheat anyone. Such people do not think about right or wrong at all, rather they only think of ways to use other people for their selfish goals.

A person who develops greed towards others' wealth, things or anything else does not remain calm. His mind is always disturbed. He uses thousands of ways to achieve that desired thing. Such a person can never be alert about his learning and wastes all his time in fulfilling his greed.

To remain lost in what has become precious to you is called greed. There is no satisfaction even after getting that thing. An avaricious man will remain so from waking up in the morning and till he closes his eyes at night. After waking up in the morning, he does everything guided by his greed. He never loses time in laughing. He will be occupied by greed all day. He will search for cheap vegetables in the vegetable market. A greedy person collects everything for the future.

As the person makes gains, his greed keeps increasing. All sins are born out of greed, which destroys all virtues. It even destroys the purity of mind. Even the very scholarly people get caught in the clutches of greed. Greed catches everyone in its clutches. Anger, respect and deceit also get subdued in front of it. Therefore, greed is not just a sin, but it is also considered to be the origin of sins. It is opposed to clean deeds.

Greediness and voracity have been considered the cause of the destruction. It is such a bad trait in a person's personality which destroys him. Greed or avarice are human faults which make a person's life painful. A greedy person is unable to live well in the present due to this bad quality as his focus becomes collecting more and more things for the future.

Many times, due to greed, man commits such a heinous crime or sin for which he has to repent. The only way to avoid greed is satisfaction; the life of a person who has attained satisfaction becomes happy and heavenly.

Acharya Chanakya has said, "The sea is never satiated even after a lot of water from the rivers reaches it. The crematorium is never satisfied even after consuming a lot of dead bodies. Even after continuously getting the food, the stomach is never full. Similarly, no matter how much you fill this pit of greed, it is never full".

He says that we must become content because a contented man is always happy. The second point is that one should fear greed because as long as there is no fear, you cannot avoid it. And thirdly, make the mind pure because the sanctification of the mind is possible only with satisfaction, by one self and with renunciation of greed.

The desire to get everything makes a person greedy.

We have a desire to own the world. Sins are committed only because of this desire. Violence, theft, robbery and attachment are all related to this feeling. For example, when you put a bucket without a base in the well, it appears full as long as it is in the well. It is empty as soon as it comes out. It seems that someone is gctting everything when he is entangled in the pleasures of the world. But as soon as the bucket comes out, there is no sign of happiness. Therefore, until the bucket of the mind does not have the base of contentment, the water of happiness cannot be filled in it. Just understand this and adopt contentment. Renounce greed.

Greed often appears filled with a desire to become rich. In fact, greed is a noose which has many aspects. Greed is basically an excessive or unrestrained desire to get more out of anything, be it money, property, power, work, or anything else.

Therefore, the student should never let the feeling of greed or avarice enter his mind. According to Acharya Chanakya, the person who has the feeling of getting or grabbing the object or the right of others is always planning for it. Such a person is unable to concentrate on his learning. So, the student should not let the feeling of greed enter his mind.

❑

6

Putting Time to Good Use

"When you begin a task, do not be afraid of failure and do not leave that task halfway. Those who work honestly are the happiest and only they make a progress."

–Chanakya

Time never stops for anyone. Therefore, each moment must be used properly. According to Acharya Chanakya, proper use of time is essential during student life. It is also necessary for students to have serious temperament with time. The student can achieve good education and success only by adopting this quality. Students who waste all their time in laughter and jokes never get the desired success.

Time travels at its own pace. It does not wait for anyone. Nobody has the power to stop it. In fact, performing the necessary and appropriate tasks on time is the best use of time. During student life, the person prepares for his future life. He strengthens himself mentally and physically. A person who is busy in other tasks and not utilizing the time properly fails in his domestic life. His future life becomes full of difficulties. He becomes physically weak. The future life of the person who makes good use of time during this period becomes free of difficulties. He continuously advances on the path of progress. Victory starts kissing his feet.

Samay labh sam labh nahin, samay chook sam chook

Chaturan chit Rahiman lagi, samay chook ki hook

The poet Rahim says that time is profit and time is also loss. Smart people take advantage of time, and if they miss it, they always have regret in their mind.

Not using time properly makes the mind fickle. Such a person cannot do any work properly. Success will run away from him. Such a person would be barbaric and cruel. He lacks a proper sense of functionality. He will neither earn knowledge nor money. He will remain a victim of unease. His life will be full of deprivations. He will become a worthy of condemnation and will have to repent in the last moments of his life; he will not gain anything even after repenting. Man should use his time wisely to take his life on the right path. He should also make his future life happy.

It is important to Keep Up with the Times

The wheel of time rotates continuously. It does not stop for anyone. Just as the sand held in a fist cannot be stopped from slipping, the wheel of time cannot be stopped. In these competitive times, it is necessary to keep up with the times. People often complain about the lack of time. Especially, the youth ignore their important work by spending their time in futile pursuits. Then they complain that they do not get time. In such a situation, time management is required. The more you do your work in an orderly manner, the better and quicker it will be.

First of all, check where you are wasting time, such as chatting, Facebook, email or television. By scheduling these tasks, you can save a lot of time.

There were two friends. Whenever one of them did any work and had a little trouble with it, he would panic and say to his other friend, "Oh brother! There is so much trouble in this. It is a very difficult task".

Another friend would listen to him and ask, "See, you have to succeed in this work, don't you?"

The first one would say, "Yes, I want to".

The other one would say, "Then go and do it. There will be no problem in this work. It is not very difficult. Even a child can do it".

Hearing this, the first friend works with enthusiasm and succeeds in it. In this way, the second person gives hope to his friend regarding his work. When his friend awakens his faith in that work, he works with double enthusiasm and succeeds.

Make Life Easier

If we work according to time management, life will become easier. Time management is very important for today's generation. They have a lot of things to do together. They have a career, friends and family. In such a situation, time will be used properly only when you have a routine.

In any case, if you finish your work on time, then it will also reduce stress and you will get enough time for sports and leisure. Otherwise, it so happens that many students spend all their time in pleasure and when the examination approaches, they think of studying instantly. But nothing happens instantly, and even if it happens, it is not very satisfying. If time management is good, then such a situation will not arrive.

Effort is Required

People are eager to achieve success and want immediate results. But most people do not want to work hard along with time management for success. Everyone wants to win, but there are very few people who have the desire to prepare to win.

Effort or exertion is the quality of a human being, on which his whole life depends. Many people spend their valuable time relying on luck but do not make any effort. If time management is combined with efforts, then it is like the icing on the cake.

Man should not rely on good luck or bad luck. He should keep doing all his work on time with time management. Otherwise, much time passes by and he is left with only one thing to say, "I was unfortunate that I could not do anything; I could not succeed".

Jaishankar Prasad has said in his play called '*Skandagupta*' -

"He who performs his deeds as the deeds of God is the incarnation of God".

That is, by doing his work on time with complete honesty, dedication and hard work, a person gets praised by everybody and is revered by all, that is, he becomes an incarnation of God. He who builds his identity based on the power of his time management is an avatar. He who is respected by all due to his qualities is an avatar. Let everyone have trust for him. He who inspires others to walk on the path of success with his virtues, his good work is the saviour. In a way, he becomes a source of inspiration for the people. Seeing him, those people who want to achieve success work like him, that is, they follow him. Thus, he is the saviour of the people, he is the incarnation. He who teaches people as to what is fair and what is unjust, he who shows others the way to succeed in life, is an avatar. One who develops all these qualities with time management is considered an avatar. One can become an incarnation by making efforts according to time.

Time Management is Victory

Time is not managed; we need to manage ourselves according to time. There will be same 24 hours. We have to prioritize our tasks according to the time. In every organization, employees have to complete their work within a stipulated time frame. Therefore, one must learn to understand the value of time and how to use it properly.

Always keep a diary with you. In this diary, you should write a fixed date and time for each of your tasks and implement it. This record will later tell you where you spent more time than necessary and where that time could be saved.

In today's time, there is no dearth of opportunities and means to prove oneself better than others and to create a special identity. But it is often seen that a person does a lot of hard work, but still is not able to achieve recognition or place according to his talent and ability.

Samay pare ochhe vachan, sab ke sahe Rahim
Sabha Dusasan pat gahe, gada liye rahe Bheem

Poet Rahim says that when the bad times arrived, he had to bear the petty and vile words, just as in a crowded assembly, Duhshasan humiliated Draupadi and the powerful Bheema who had his mace in hand could not protect Draupadi.

Avoiding Excuses

You must have often heard people say that they want to do so much, but that the lack of time is creating hindrances. But while saying this, they probably forget that everyone has twenty-four hours in a day. No one has more or less than that. Then how can anyone complain about the lack of time? The only difference is that someone makes maximum use of these twenty-four hours and someone cries about the lack of time.

It is not that people who think that the twenty-four hours of the day are insufficient are afraid to work hard. However, they also have to understand that it is very difficult to achieve success with hard work alone. Proper management of time and personal discipline can make the road to success a lot easier.

By properly managing the time, we can not only increase our efficiency, but other important tasks which get left behind by us due to lack of time can also be completed easily. Time management can get you success. At the same time, if you waste time, it can cause stress as well as distract your attention from the goal. Plan one day in advance what important tasks you have to do tomorrow and how much time you have to spend on them so that you can complete other tasks easily. The biggest benefit from this will be that you will also get your priorities clear and at the same time you will also learn to complete the work in the stipulated time.

Make a Diary

Make a diary. Write in it how you spend your day. By doing this, you will know how much time you have given to non-essential work. When you assess yourself when you are alone, you will definitely be able to recognize your shortcomings. Keep in mind that there is nothing bigger in this world than time, which you should spend with full understanding and maturity.

Rich or poor, teenager or old, child or young, everyone has 24 hours. It depends on you how you use those 24 hours. If you want to get rich or succeed in life, then understand the value of time. Do not let it go waste. Use every moment of time wisely.

According to Shakespeare, lose the opportunity today by wasting time, the same thing will happen tomorrow, and then there will be more lethargy.

According to Charles Darwin, a person who dares to waste an hour, does not understand the value of life.

According to Franklin, do not waste time because it is the building element of life. There is a saying in English – Time and tide do not wait for anyone.

Time is the Biggest Wealth

It is written in *Chanakya Neeti*: The time of a wise person is spent in the pursuit of poetry, art and science, while the time of a foolish person is spent in sleep or discord. Time is changing from moment to moment. If you do not understand the importance of time, then it will not value you. Every second is important in life. The importance of time can be told by the student who has failed in his class. He will have to sit in the same class again for a year to pass. Similarly, ask the player about the importance of time, who could not get the medal because he was late by one second. If you want to achieve success in life, then you have to understand the value of every moment of time. Those who lost time was as if they lost everything. The plants of success plants grow only in the field of time.

Samay paay fal hota hai, samay paay jhari jaat
Sada rahai nahin ek si, ka Rahim pachhtaat

Poet Rahim says that according to time, the tree has fruit at its fixed time and falls according to the time. Time is never the same. So, never worry during bad times.

Chanakya says that time is the greatest wealth. Until we understand the value of time, we will not be able to become rich. To become rich, one has to be aware of the value of time. Generate the ability to do more work in less time and complete the work at the right time. Then you can get ahead of time. Time management is considered to be the key to becoming rich. The person who has found this key is fortunate indeed. He will be able to open the treasure chest of Kubera. Successful life is a series of successful days, hours and minutes.

Time is Money

One has to understand that time is money. Every moment has to be considered precious. Time should not be allowed to go waste. The value of time has to be recovered. Only then you can join the list of successful people. For this, time management is most important. Without this, a lot of your precious time is wasted. You have to develop time management yourself. You can do this according to your time, work and personality. The little formula is that firstly one has to understand the value of time, secondly one has to save time, and thirdly one has to cultivate time.

The Value of Time

Remember, time is a kind of priceless wealth. The destroyed material wealth can be recovered, but the lost time cannot be recovered. Time should be spent more thoughtfully than money.

Keeping in mind your priorities for twenty-four hours of day and night, the work will have to be scheduled according to minimum and maximum time. You take care of your minutes, hours will take care of themselves.

Deal with every task. Do not defer. Do not let the opportunity slip. Instead of complaining about lack of time, cultivate it. That is, do what you can to change your 24 hours into 48 hours. Swett Marden says, "God gives one moment at a time, and takes that moment away before giving another". So -

Kaal kare so aaj kar, aaj kare so ab
Pal mein pralay hoegi, bahuri karega kab

Sir Walter Rayleigh was asked by a man, "How do you get so much work done in such a short time?"

He replied, "Whatever work I have, I finish it immediately. Whatever work you have, finish it immediately. Do not wait. Also, whatever work you do, always do it carefully. A lot of time gets wasted if the work is done carelessly. Do not undertake too many tasks at once. Many problems arise when you do many things together, due to which none of them is likely to be completed on time".

Do Everything on Time

Many of us are forgetful. We remember the tasks while leaving the house in the morning, but on our way home in the evening, we forget what work we had to do. Many times, we miss many good opportunities by not working on time. Keep in mind that if you want to excel in your field of work, then you will have to make a list of all your tasks according to time. By doing this, you will remember what important work you have to do and at what time.

Time-table

- Include the complete routine in the time-table.
- Every task should be given enough time.
- Going to sleep early and getting up early is imperative.

- Ensure that you get at least six hours of sleep.
- Do not avoid exercise or sports at all.
- Instead of reading books of all subjects on a single day, set different days for each subject.
- Keep in mind that everything you read should be understood.
- Time-table should be practical.
- Do not take the time-table as a challenge, rather maintain some flexibility.
- The basic purpose of the time-table is to regularize and organize the studies. Therefore, while making the time-table, keep in mind that its original purpose should be fulfilled.
- Entertainment is very important to keep the mind fresh. It is also necessary to give place to entertainment in the time-table. If your routine goes awry, then there is no need to be frustrated or upset. As soon as the situation is normal, again follow the time-table.

Balancing Time Management

Some practical tips that will help a student in balancing time management -

- Give enough time for planning time management. It has been said that failing to plan is to plan for failure.
- Set goals at different levels (e.g., annual, quarterly, monthly, weekly and daily), and make a written phased planning programme to achieve them.
- Make proper use of the time of each day and plan on the previous day itself. This will be effective in preventing waste of time.
- Man, being an intelligent creature, can continuously think of so many tasks that he can never complete. Set your priorities. Think carefully about what to do first, what to do later and what never to do.

- Schedule the use of television, internet, social websites strictly. We do not realize the time that we waste on them. Avoid receiving/checking updates on mobile/computer frequently. Not only does it waste time, but you are also not able to concentrate properly on the work at hand. This has a huge adverse effect on your efficiency.
- Just as the effect of bathing gradually fades from the body and we have to bathe daily, the effect of inspiration from the mind also gradually fades. Therefore, make sure to take time every day for some kind of religious-spiritual inspiration so that you can always continue on the path of self-progress.
- Take proper care of physical health as well. Make sure to keep aside at least half an hour to one hour daily for outdoor sports, physical exercise, yoga and pranayama, excursions etc. Remember, many youths acquire unlimited wealth by sacrificing their physical health, but later even after spending all that money, it is not possible to recover good physical health.
- Even if you are not able to follow the planned programme set out in the beginning, do not get discouraged and continue making effort. 100 percent adherence to the plan should be your goal. So, keep making effort to adhere to the goal increasingly and gradually.
- It has become the nature of most of us that we ignore the good and get frustrated by paying more attention to the bad. A lot of good is happening around us. Ignore the bad, be free of all prejudices and focus your attention on goodness and positivity. You will find that there will be a gradual increase in the goodness and positivity around you.

Tomorrow Never Comes

Tomorrow means the next day which never comes and always remains tomorrow. Many people have the habit of always depending on tomorrow to do any work saying that they will do it tomorrow. Sometimes in human life there are many such moments which benefit the person, that is, those moments make him successful. But whom? Only those who realize that opportunity and take advantage of it. And those who leave it for tomorrow keep waiting for it.

Suppose, you have to do some work at ten o'clock this morning. You wait for the clock to strike ten o'clock. While waiting, your mind gets entangled in other things. When it's ten o'clock, you wonder why do it now, I will do it tomorrow, while that work should have been done today because after today, it will be ten o'clock only the next day.

Similarly, in the life of man, when there are moments of progress on the path of success and achievement, then he should be catch them immediately. If we miss ten o'clock today, it will again be ten o'clock the next day. But if you miss an opportunity today, you do not know when those moments of success will again come into your life. The time of opportunity is not fixed and such opportunities are let go by those who do not want to do anything in life. But those who achieve success do not postpone such opportunities to tomorrow; rather they wait day and night for such moments and grab them as soon as they are seen.

Time Management Brings Confidence

Self-confidence is the weapon through which we can easily do the biggest thing easily, that is, we can achieve the greatest success. One who does not lack confidence continues to earn successes in life. Self-confidence is the strong fort in front of which armed men also become helpless. When we achieve success in a task with our confidence, then the same confidence again works towards success. In this way, our confidence increases and it becomes natural for us, that is, it becomes our nature. Confidence comes from time management.

The key to confidence is to be optimistic, not pessimistic because where there is hope to achieve success, there is confidence to do that work. When one is optimistic, qualities like enthusiasm, efficiency, courage, etc., come naturally because these qualities increase confidence in human beings. On the contrary, pessimism gives rise to many negativities. When one is pessimistic, there is always a doubt in human mind about doing any work, "Will I will be able to do this work or not? What kind of troubles will come while doing this work?", etc.; many such doubts bother him. Because of these doubts, he is not able to perform easy tasks and starts to panic even while doing small tasks. This indicates man's lack of confidence and he is unsuccessful. His steps falter and he reaches the abysmal depths. That is, he keeps wandering in the labyrinth; he wanders and returns to the starting point. On the contrary, when a person does all the work with time management, his confidence will not waver.

Carelessness about Time is a Costly Deal

This deficiency is found in those who are careless about time – those who neither want to succeed, nor know the way to achieve success. Those people suffer due to failure, and they can also affect their environment adversely. They only take, they do not give back anything to anyone. Giving means that they are unable to do such work which can act as inspiration for others. Taking means that they take only negativities, they are not able to learn anything from the success of others. Gradually they are destroyed and there is no one who would remember their name in this world. But if we look at its other aspects, then the self-confident people not only succeed themselves, they also leave inspiration for others in this world in the form of their actions, and that motivation is accepted only by those who have the passion to achieve success.

Many times, you must have seen that people drive motorcycles in the well of death in fairs. How do they do this? It is because of their confidence. Many people jump into the well of death by offering themselves to fire. How do they do this? It is because they have full confidence that they will complete this task as they have managed the time. They know that even a moment's lapse can lead to their death.

Many times, you must have seen that a person standing in a lion's cage in a circus, tricks dangerous lions with only a hunter in his hand. This is due to time management and confidence. At the same time, due to management and self-confidence, courage is instilled in him and he is able to perform such exciting feats. On seeing them, those people who lack time management and confidence are filled with surprise. But the truth is that we can aslo do this work because they are also ordinary people like us. We can do all this by instilling confidence within ourselves and managing time.

Sometimes these people who perform exciting adventures also get defeated. But when their confidence staggers and they miss time management, then an accident takes place. Therefore, it is needed that we should always build our confidence and make time management the axis of life.

If we look at the life of any successful person, then we will find their time management and self-confidence at work behind their success. They do not let any doubt arise in their mind while doing any work. They only have a strong belief in their mind that they have to achieve success in this task.

One who awakens his hidden power of time management knows that now he will be successful in whatever he does. He never worries about what problems will arise when doing this work or what people will say. He is just focused that he has to succeed. In the face of his unshakable confidence, his friends, his critics, his enemies also bow down or become his companions.

Once upon a time, Striven who was a just and wise man was approached by a person and asked, "What would you do if someone attacked you?"

Striven replied, "I will do nothing".

The person was surprised to hear that. He asked, "Why would you not do anything?"

Striven said, "My castle is very safe. Its walls are fortified. No one can break them. That's why I won't do anything".

The man was again amazed and said, "Your castle! When did you build the castle? Where is your castle?"

Striven said, “Brother, my time management and confidence is my castle, which few people have and one who has the castle of time management and confidence never feels insecure. He will always be safe. So, nobody can attack me”.

When that person saw Striven’s confidence, he bowed down to him. In fact, that person was the head of the rival army and had come there to attack Striven. But seeing Striven’s confidence, he quietly returned from there without attacking him.

So, time management and self-confidence make the task easy, which we do not even expect. Man flying airplanes, flying rockets, reaching the moon, etc. are all the results of time management and confidence.

Success stories can be read clearly on the faces of the people who have time management and self-confidence. His joyful face will look different. Conversely, a man who lacks time management will appear surrounded by doubts and disappointments. There will never be a smile of success on his face.

The value of the person who works with time management increases in the society. He becomes a source of inspiration for other people. People start seeing him as a hero. His success story is not hidden from anyone. They become people’s ideals. But for which people? Only for those who themselves want to do something, who want to achieve success in life.

Time managers influence people with the effect of their powerful voice. There is enthusiasm in their speech by which they endear themselves to others by filling them with the same enthusiasm and passion. About such people, unsuccessful people say, “He is one person who can do anything. He has great confidence”.

Understand the Limits of Time

All the secrets of life are contained in the glory and limit of time. Every moment of time is valuable. Every moment is precious. Time is an infinite stream created by moment-by-moment drops, in which life flows continuously. No moment of time is ordinary. It is unusual and wonderful, because it was a moment that gave us life. It is only a moment that grants success and failure. Every moment brings a unique opportunity. The true meaning lies only in the good use of the moment. The chaotic lifestyle and negative habits burn down valuable occasions like Holi. It destroys or complicates the means by which success can be achieved.

It is said that a good friend is a good guide because such friends help us in difficult situations and increase our courage. But unfortunately, such true friends are rarely found in the present environment and the result is that we are surrounded by friends who instead of helping us with our problems create problems for us. To be honest, the circle of friends is the easiest way to waste time. Therefore, if we are thinking seriously about making good use of our time, then we have to work with wisdom and discretion in the selection of our friends. First of all, we have to reduce the number of our friends and secondly, we have to be very careful about the selection of our good friends.

Keep Track of Time

Have you ever pondered over how much of our precious time we waste on television, internet and Facebook etc.? In reality, when we watch television, the biggest problem is that we do not know how much time has been spent. As the modern incarnation of the information revolution, the Internet and mobile have brought many miracles into our lives. However, as we have got caught up in their colourful world, what we have lost is time. But it does not mean that we should stay away from the world of television and internet. However, we should try to make sure that we take care of time while watching television or while working on the internet, otherwise precious time slips from our hands just like sand slips from the fist and we will not even know.

Waste of Time

In fact, if we are always dedicated and passionate towards fulfilling our dreams, then there is no doubt that we can use both our life and time in a miraculous way. The famous Hindi litterateur Premchand once said that I wasted time and now time is ruining me, i.e., wasting time is like wasting life. For success, ambitious people should first develop the habit of doing their work at the right time.

Best Use of Time

The latest research shows that the left side of the brain has analytical intelligence, while the right side has imagination which plays an essential role in the planning of time. The cognition of time related to both parts of the brain can be utilized well. In this modern scientific discovery, the mantras of the Upanishads are reflected. In these mantras, it has been said that due to strong willpower and strong determination, the time cycle can be forced to change as per our will.

Nowadays, the importance of time and its management has increased a lot. This is because the corporate world is emphasizing on more productivity in a short period of time with respect to economy. This is intelligence. The importance of time has also been accepted in the spiritual world. Time management means using time appropriately and meaningfully according to the situation. The rule of time is – continuous, unceasing flow. Let this truth be understood that we too are flowing in this stream. So, we should learn to use our time, days, months and years properly. An action plan should be made, in which there should be an opportunity to use each day and every moment along with each year purposefully. Keep in mind that the action plan should not be one-sided. Rather it should be multidimensional. In this, right from our thinking, character and behaviour, the rules of the family and society should be presented in complete harmony with the times.

Good Sense

People come and people go, but time always continues without stopping for anyone. We never catch hold of time. The more we follow it, the more it moves ahead. It is very strange that despite knowing the importance of time we waste it. The root cause of this is our inability of 'time management'. We forget that managing time is very important for life management or else chaos prevails in our lives. Good time management depends on good understanding. Until we do not understand this resource properly, we will not be able to use it properly.

As mentioned earlier, we all have equal amount of time. There is no rich or poor in this matter. But who, how much and how well this time is used depends on their understanding and wisdom.

Find out in which tasks we waste our time. Many personal problems like lack of planning, not being able to delegate work to others, various obstacles, jealousy, hatred, anger waste a lot of our time unnecessarily. To avoid all this, Kabir's formula is useful for us – Kaal kare so aaj kar.

Time does not Wait for Anyone

There is a saying, time and sea tides do not wait for anyone. Time is never short or less. Only the right balance has to be established.

Many people get up late in the morning. Their day starts late. How can it be good for you to spend these morning hours called Amritvela in sleeping? Human beings should get complete sleep, but there is no point in continuing to lie in the bed needlessly. Just as keeping awake late at night is harmful, waking up late in the morning is also not a sign of good health. When the new day starts in the morning, then the mind, brain and organs of human beings are filled with energy and enthusiasm. There is concentration. More work is done in less time and there are few errors.

Do not blame time, do not make excuse about the lack of time. Learn to control the time. Do not let time dominate you. If you change a little, then you will see that there is no shortage of time. You will have plenty of time in your hands. Your bag is always full of time. Learn to appreciate time. One who does not appreciate time, time does not appreciate them; leaving him behind, it moves forward.

Proper Use of Time

Acharya Chanakya says that we cannot tie time within boundaries, but by organizing ourselves according time, we can definitely imagine touching the sky. The waste of time not only disorganizes our lives, it also proves to be a hindrance in the path of our dreams, our destination, our hopes. Proper use of time is the best means to adapt time to your dreams.

Proper use of time or time management plays a special role in the art of living. Everyone desires to achieve the objective, but he does not know how inaccessible and full of difficulties this path to achieving the objectives is. We are not aware that we can achieve these goals by organizing our life. Life is organized with time management. This is the only means which motivates man towards his objectives.

There is no Shortcut to Success

Today, the biggest problem of the younger generation is dreaming of achieving maximum benefits in a short time with little effort, or we can say that fulfilling their objectives through shortcuts. This path only leads man to the abysmal depths. By adopting this path, the person deceives himself, and at the same time he also forgets whether the path that he has chosen is right or wrong.

Finishing the tasks hastily within a time line can be harmful. While handling the task, we may forget to notice if the process of completing the work has been followed properly or not. Due to this, it would be difficult to get the desired results. Lack of time management awakens our tendency to postpone our work or decision. Gradually, we become lazy or we can say that we become long-sighted, which can distract us from our objectives. Time management prevents unnecessary time wastage. Also, it does not let the efforts made for the work go in vain. Hence, time management is considered to be a guarantee of success.

The Essential Principles of Time Management

The following things should be specially kept in mind for best time management:

- You should have a diary in which to prepare a list of decisions and a description of the time period to complete it.
- Prioritize some of your decisions and plan accordingly.
- When you are busy in accomplishing your objectives, then do not waste your precious time in fulfilling the objective of others, and politely refuse the person.
- After making your list of tasks, distribute those tasks to your colleagues on the basis of their ability and competence.
- Keep a plan for each day's activities ready and accordingly, take the initiative.
- Avoid interruptions in the middle of work, such as the phone ringing repeatedly. If possible, then find a secluded place and implement your efforts.
- Take complete care of diet and exercise and get full sleep so that you can stay fresh.
- Do not get distracted during tasks, and complete your work with a focused mind.
- If necessary, consult your subordinates or colleagues and achieve your goal.
- Sometimes when you do not find yourselves mentally or physically competent, then seek the solution to these problems by consulting a psychologist or experts and then execute the plan.
- Read articles and books on management and success topics from time to time.
- Participate in workshops on management and make yourself aware of new ideas so that you can stay updated.
- Study the research being done on management, see their results and execute them.
- Read about the life and struggles of the most successful personalities of the world and know what is the right way to succeed.

- Study the reports of surveys conducted from time to time.
- Do not violate your deadline.
- Give yourself time and do self-analysis.
- Determine whether the work you have taken in hand is leading you to proper results or not.
- Make a plan before doing any work.
- Walk in step with time.

In today's world, people have to multitask. Time given for completing a job is short. In such a situation, there is a lot of struggle for time. Since the number of tasks in life cannot be reduced and the hours available during the day cannot be increased, with time management we can increase our efficiency and achieve success.

Therefore, it is important to focus on time management. We feel the passage of time. So, it is in our hands to use it.

All the power of time is limited to the present. Our future is secured by focusing on the present. From one point of view, despite being valuable like money, time is not like money because it cannot be held. Whenever we get time, we have to use it immediately. The time that passes once is gone forever. That is why we can remember the past, but we cannot regain it.

The speed of time is subjective and relative. Depending on their circumstances, the time spent during an hour is short for someone. If we are not working or are working in an disinterested way, then the time that elapses is very long. But it seems extremely short when we are working with concentration.

Past Time does not Come Back

It is important for us to take cognizance of whether the work is going on as planned. If necessary, a revision of the plan should be carried out periodically to finish the work within the time limit. It is not necessary that new ideas should be completely new. Many times, a lot of time is spent in the process of innovating or appearing new and we forget the time limit. Remember that the combination of two ideas can also be the originator of innovation.

Every Moment is Valuable

Time is the most precious thing in this world. But we also waste it the most. The reason is that we cannot understand the value of each moment.

Since our childhood till our youth, a big part time of is spent in learning, whose returns are manifold when we grow up. If you have given less time to learning, then the rest of your life you will have to spend much more time. Therefore, whenever you would want to save time in the future then you would have to spend it first. If you don't do it, then you will have to pay a very big price. Therefore, in whatever field you work, give enough time to learning better, do not hold back on it at all. It is said that if time is with you, you can conquer the world. But the time does not support anyone just like that. It values us only when we value it.

Importance of Time

Proper utilization and proper management of time are essential elements for achieving success in any area of life. By ignoring time, no person can climb a single step of success. So far, all the great men in the world who have created the criteria for success have understood the importance of time well. One second of promptness makes you victorious while a second's lapse results in defeat.

Time is often compared to money. A person is able to use his money better only when he invests it because only then he is in a position to spend it better in the future. For the betterment of future, investment of time is also necessary.

Time management is an art. Before understanding that, it is necessary to know how a person wastes his precious time. The main factors of time wastage are – lack of proper list of tasks and prioritization, trying to handle multiple tasks at the same time, being busy with uncontrolled telephone calls, not using a diary, meeting friends without a predetermined plan, having a tendency to postpone tasks, and not developing a habit of saying 'No'.

Life is a journey and time is in motion. Therefore, there should be a clear identification of what we have to do and what we should not do. In addition, knowledge of the energy cycle is necessary along with the identification of one's own potential. You can become the master of your time if you constantly work on some essential principles. Keep your goal in front of you, prioritize, use technology that simplifies your work, finish the task about which you had thought first, keep aside some free time to increase your efficiency, always keep your writing pad with you, make a clear distinction between urgent and necessary tasks, avoid the habit of always saying 'Yes', manage your stress, keep your study area clean and organized, give some time to organize yourself every day and also be clear about your nearest and distant goal.

Therefore, the only secret of individual and collective success is worshipping the time, that is, utilizing each moment. If we can turn every moment into a lamp of means, then our life will be auspicious and we can easily achieve any goal without doubt.

In the Atharvaveda, time has been called horse. Just as the horse moves at a fast pace, the time also passes speedily. Just as the sun shines with seven colours, time also shines brightly in the world. Just as the power of the sun is predominant in the world, the importance of time is also recognized in the world. Time is always young and novel and the same. Time never gets old. Time has bound all the functions of the world within the border. Except God, soul and nature, all other things are bound with time. Time is the same towards all beings. It only waits for opportunity. It destroys only those creatures whose time has come to an end.

When the body becomes fragile due to old age with time, then no one has the ability to do any work. Then the human form gives up the life and leaves. When the whole world sleeps, time stays awake. The power of time is amazing and great. Lost wealth and health, forgotten knowledge, lost empire can be recovered, but the time that has passed can never return.

Time is Precious Wealth

The wealth of time is more important than the money. So, do not waste time. He who takes advantage of the present moment builds his future. God has not been partial in distributing the wealth of time. This wealth is same for everyone. All things in the world have value. But time is priceless and it is considered to be the mine of all good qualities. Money is important, but the wealth of time is valuable. The natural system of the world teaches us to follow time. The sun, the moon, the movement of the earth, the change in seasons – all these indicate that we should follow the time and discipline. Time and not money is the basis of our life. Therefore, human life becomes meaningful only by walking in step with time which is in a state of constant movement. Time is life, time is progress, time is the step to climb to the highest peak of greatness.

Time is the key to success. The wheel of time is working at its own pace or rather it is running. Often, we get to hear from people around us that they do not get time at all. In fact, we are unable to walk in step with the constantly moving time and lag behind. Despite having a storehouse of valuable wealth like time, we always complain about the lack of it because we spend the precious time thoughtlessly.

Elapsed Time and Spoken Words

Waste of time is the biggest enemy in the path of development. According to Chanakya, the time that is wasted never returns. Our prized present gradually becomes a ghost, which never returns. There is a saying – elapsed time and spoken words can never come back.

No work should be postponed to tomorrow because if we keep postponing today's work to tomorrow and so on, that will increase the workload for today, tomorrow and so on. Stale work will become distasteful like stale food. Precious wealth like time cannot be stored like gold and silver because it is in constant motion. We have right over it only if we use it properly, otherwise it is destroyed. The use of time is more important than the use of money because the happiness of all of us depends on it.

According to Chanakya, a person who does not take care of time in life experiences only failure and regret. Time is a valuable element and it does not return, but we often do not understand its importance. But those who understand its importance will always be known in the history of the world.

Ishwar Chandra Vidyasagar was always punctual. When he would go to college, the vendors on the street used to set the time in their watches upon seeing him. Galileo used to sell medicines. Taking some time out of that activity, he made many scientific inventions. Despite being busy with running a household, Harriet Witcher Stow wrote a hard-hitting book against slavery, 'Tom Uncle's Cabin', which is praised even today as an unmatched classic. What it means is that there is one thing in common among all the developing and progressive people – the proper use of time.

The Time Cycle is Regular in Nature

Time management is best understood in nature. The time cycle is regular in nature. Day and night, the seasons come and go on time. If there is any irregularity, then the nature demonstrates destruction as well. Many times, ignoring the time turns victory into defeat. Napoleon defeated Austria because her troops were delayed by five minutes. But in a few minutes, Napoleon was taken captive because one of his commanders was late. The biggest reason for Napoleon's defeat in the Battle of Waterloo was the disregard for time. It is said that lost wealth can still be earned, forgotten learning can be discovered again, but the lost time cannot be brought back and only regret remains.

In the womb of time, there is a treasure trove of wealth. But it is found by only those who use it properly. Japanese citizens do something interesting. When they get free from their professional work, they regularly make a new toy or machine from the parts of small machines or toy. They get extra money from this work. The biggest reason for their prosperity is the productive use of time.

Samarth Guru Swami Ramdas used to say – *Ek sadaiv panachau lakshan | Rikama jau ne do ek kshan*. This means that a man who makes good use of time and does not waste even a single moment is very fortunate.

Time is a ladder for reaching the highest peak. The palace of life is made of bricks of time, hours and minutes. Nature did not make anyone rich or poor. It has shared its valuable wealth i.e., twenty-four hours equally with all people. No matter how hard-working a person is, but his work is wasted if it's not done on time. According to Chanakya, crops that are not harvested on time are destroyed. The untimely sown seed goes waste. Each moment of life brings the possibility of a bright future. We wouldn't know if the moment we are wasting considering it as meaningless could be a moment of good luck for us. The approaching moment is like Akashkusum. You should fill yourself with its fragrance.

Life was Created by Time

Franklin said – Do not waste time because life is made of time itself. It would not be an exaggeration to say that time and ocean waves do not wait for anyone. It is our duty to make full use of time.

Time is Life

Time has been considered as life. It is said that if you are wasting time, then you are wasting your life; if you are making good use of time, then you are making your life good.

A saint asked his disciples, "What is the most important thing in life that we should never lose nor use it wrongly? Because after losing it, even God cannot get it back for us".

All the disciples gave different answers such as money, love, parents, family, patience, courage, strength, knowledge, devotion, teacher, God and breath, saying that these are most important. But his most beloved disciple said, "Time is most important and we can get everything back except breath. We will have to stop breathing at some point. Only time is that important thing in life which we should never lose because after losing it no one can bring it back for us. There is only time in the world which every person has got in a limited amount, everything else can be unlimited".

Exam Dirst

According to Chanakya, time is a cycle that does not stop for anyone nor does it come back for anyone. It is said that time is very strange; if we go along with it, luck changes, and if we do not, then it changes the luck itself. Time is considered to be the strongest thing in this world created by God. When it changes, then it can turn a pauper into a king and a king into a pauper. Time is also a good doctor; it is capable of healing the biggest wound. Time has also been considered a good teacher. It always teaches us; in school, we have to take exams after learning. But time takes our test first and then teaches.

To be successful in life, it is necessary to perform tasks at a certain time because time does not wait for anyone. Therefore, it is very important to use the time properly. One minute cannot change our life; however, a decision taken in one minute can change our life. The importance of time also varies for everyone.

Time and Wisdom

Time and wisdom are available only to the lucky people because often one does not get wisdom on time and when one gets it, it's too late. You can use the time to succeed in the following ways -

Only by being punctual can you succeed. That is why it is important to do every task on time.

In today's competitive era, in many places, time is the only measure of success. For example, school and college examinations, national and international sports and big projects given with time in view – all of them have to be finished in a limited time given to us.

That means, to be successful, whatever work we have to do, it not only has to be done neatly and cleanly but we also have to finish it on time. Earlier it was said that people do not remember how quickly you work, but they definitely remember how well you do it. But today the perception has changed. Today it is said - 'No matter how good the work done is compared to others, it is of no importance if it is not done on time.'

Admissions to many courses and jobs are given till a particular age. That is also why we can say that we cannot succeed by wasting time. Out of the main three components of success – hard work, determination and dedication, hard work will require a lot of time and without hard work you can never succeed.

In order to be successful, we have to do a lot of work and we have to arrange the tasks and the time available to us in such a way that all the work gets done on time. For that, we have to adjust our work with the time we have and we have to finish all the work by doing the necessary work first. It is often said that a person does not get tired due to workload but he gets tired because it is disorganized. It is said that doing one thing at a time is the simplest way to do a lot of work.

Only a man who starts work on time can finish it on time. It is said that only two types of people fail in life – one, those who think but do not start work on time and the other, those who work but never think. That is to say, a thoughtless task can also be a reason for failure. So, whatever you do, do it thoughtfully and on time.

Being True to Time

Only by understanding time can we understand ourselves. One who does not understand the importance of time cannot succeed for sure. Realizing the importance of time, there is a pleasure in carrying out the work in a truthful manner. By measuring the circumference of time, when you showcase your talent, its enjoyment increases even more. Our fundamental and natural abilities are our qualifications. Understand them and know the art of using them in full truth and honesty as required.

Not exercising our abilities faithfully is like standing with your hands tied despite knowing everything. Time has an important role in any task from start to finish. If we do not understand the importance of time in today's fast paced world, challenges and competition, then believe that you will lag behind others.

When we used to read about the importance of time during our student life, we often used to have a lot of time. As a result, we did not understand the importance of time. After spending a lot of time, we now realize that time is valuable. The tasks that can be performed happily when done with awareness about time seeming big and complex if we lose time.

Make a list of some of your tasks that you have been avoiding and, in the end, either you had to leave them or you completed them half-heartedly. You can also see that you incurred a direct loss due the work you gave up, and the work that you did half-heartedly could not create your image and influence as desired.

Life is very subtle and is working at a great intensity. Each approaching moment brings a message of new possibilities and new responsibilities for us. If we are not able to fulfil our old obligations in time, then how will we be able to take up new responsibilities? The person who postpones today's work can see neither his today nor tomorrow. Understanding the importance of time is the first characteristic of any successful person.

One who does not understand the importance of time, time also does not understand his importance. All the people who have succeeded in their life had only 24 hours a day. Louis Pasteur, Abraham Lincoln, Mahatma Gandhi, Michelangelo, Albert Einstein, Thomas Alva Edison, Indira Gandhi, Bill Gates, Dhirubhai Ambani, J. R. D. Tata – you name any one, every one of them created new records of success in their life by using these 24 hours. It is true that we all have only 24 hours. But if you look honestly, do we use them in the true sense? Probably not.

During the course of our life, many times, we have to organize time and at other times, we have to mould ourselves according to the trend of time. We also have to face many situations in our daily life which we really have no control over, such as sleep, eating and other activities of our daily life. Many of these activities naturally take a number of hours from our 24 hours to complete. Out of 24 hours, if we spend 10 hours a day in bathing, eating, sleeping, etc., then we have only 14 hours left. You can also understand that we have control over only 58 percent of the time while 42 percent of the time keeps running at its natural pace. On an average, each person lives till the age of 70. During these 70 years, he spends 35 years sleeping because half of them were nights. Out of these 35 years, till the age of 20, he often does not have knowledge of good or bad. Now there are 15 years remaining.

It means we have got very little time to do what we want to do in life. 15 × 365 = 5,475 days.

Doing more than one task at a time is like killing many birds with one stone. Actually, a lot of our time is wasted in useless things. There are many tasks where we have to stop midway while doing them or we have to wait for someone else due to the nature of the task. In such a scenario, in order to make the best use of our time, we should make a list of our tasks every day -

- Essential Work
- Very important work
- Important work
- Things to do

Write your list in a small diary. Keep looking in the diary during your daily routine. Carry out the tasks that you have written in the list of Essential Work first. Then deal with the Most importantwWork followed by importantwWork. In this list, also write down the names of some people whom you have to telephone. These days, aphone is a facility which is usually available to all. In today's active life, aphone has also become an important medium for carrying out many of our tasks. Whenever we get time, we can take stock of the progress of our work through a phone or give necessary directions to the concerned persons on it.

There are some things that we have to do, but their priority is not fixed. We can put them in the list of Things to do and we can tackle them as and when we get time. The principle of doing many things at the same time also teaches us to save time.

Those who wish to make good use of time should follow the natural messages and according to that determine their routine and working style. By neglecting nature, we cannot establish a real balance between our time and body. A person who sleeps early and rises early in the morning is a healthy, fortunate and knowledgeable person.

Controlling Time

People moving with the times have always been considered smart. Punctuality is important for everyone. Getting late even by a short time means the entire routine will be disturbed. People who complain that even 24 hours are less do not really keep up with the times. This is the reason that time leaves them behind. If someone wakes up late in the morning (around 8 am), then it is obvious that his routine will be surely affected.

For example, as soon as he leaves his bed, he starts worrying about reaching office. As a result, he gets busy preparing without losing a single moment. He hurriedly freshens up and leaves for work with whatever he finds. So, there is a feeling of fatigue and tiredness at the beginning of the day itself. This is where failure starts. Acharya Chanakya says that one should practice waking up before dawn. To make life spirited and enjoyable, make a habit of getting up between five to six in the morning. In the beginning, if you cannot wake up, then take the help of a responsible family member or an alarm clock. Many health problems have become common today due to irregular lifestyle and bad food habits. After getting up in the morning, make a habit of exercising, too. With this, your body will also remain fit and you will be able to do your work with concentration.

You should decide what should control your time. Be careful while scheduling your time. It is best to set a time and follow it. Give time the highest importance in your life. The goal setting opportunities do not always come in life. Here, it is very important to know that once you enter the wrong path, every step goes in the wrong direction. Just as when one button of the shirt is tied wrong, all the other buttons also seem wrong, whatever path a man chooses, good or bad, the journey for the rest of his life is also decided in the same direction.

People who are unable to control their time create many difficulties for themselves. One of the main reasons for not being able to control the time is our disordered lifestyle. The most common example of mismanaged functioning is not finding the required papers or files on time in office. According to a survey, different people working in an office waste almost half an hour every day in searching a paper or file. Due to haste or apathy, we are unable to develop the habit of putting things in proper places and then when we need them, we waste a lot of our time finding them.

Stop Postponing

We are made only by the work we do. Ultimately, our work is what makes us. If you see, people address us by our profession or the work that we do throughout our life. The person practising medicine is called doctor and the person practising law is called lawyer. Their qualities, cast, religion, etc. come later. We learn something new every moment and increase our resources. People who perform tasks at the right time also perform tasks that seem impossible.

Remember, a man is not valued by the things that he has but by the person he is. George Catholil used to say that God created man and appointed him as his associate in his constantly evolving creation. According to the basic plan of God, man also has to keep creating every moment, making himself and his world perfect.

The goals of people who keep avoiding their work are never fulfilled. Those who roam around and waste their precious time, who work without thinking, who start the work but leave it unfinished and move on to other tasks when they face struggle arising from crisis, obstruction, those who do not have the ability to complete any task are not able to succeed anywhere and anytime.

According to our requirement and needs, we can draw the time-table. Keeping in mind the nature and routine of our work, we can create three types of time tables – detailed, medium and concise:

- **Six Hours** - Sleep and Rest.
- **Two Hours** - Bath and Meditation.
- **Two hours** - Tea, breakfast and snacks.
- **Two hours** - For family and children.
- **Two hours** - Newspaper, television or reading of books.
- **One hour** - Social activities, ceremonies, seminars, gatherings, etc.
- **One hour** - Time spent in traffic to and from office.
- **Eight hours** - Work, job, business, etc.

There is only one way to stay put in this world of globalization - to keep moving forward. And to grow, it is necessary that we know our destination and also get an idea of the difficulties that would come in our way. In such a situation, we can move ahead only with time management. But always keep in mind that everything in life will not go according to you. We often face such situations in our life.

Until you understand your value, you will not understand the importance of your time. Unless you understand the importance of your time, you will not do anything about it. As long as you are not determined to achieve anything in your professional and personal life, you will remain an ordinary person following a certain pattern in the crowd. If you want to achieve anything in life, then you have to set new goals and achieve them.

Time is great and nothing is stronger than time. Time never bows or bends nor stops nor waits for anyone. At the same time, time is such a doctor who heals every wound. Therefore, learn to worship time and respect it at all times. It is said that if time is with you, you can bend the whole world. But time does not support anyone easily. As long as we respect it, it respects us. So -

- Work according to your need and time.
- Do every work on time.
- Keep in touch with people.
- Share your work.

- Choose the right job.
- Utilize free time.
- Respect time.
- It is better if every task is performed with concentration.

Reflect upon yourself and remove the problems going on in your mind. Internal conflicts complicate your perception of time. It is a very pleasant feeling when you know how much time you have for yourself. Draw a picture of achievements and bitter experiences of the past as well as a picture of your future in your mind. This will help you bring your priorities into a rhythm. The synergy of internal organization and external organization is very important.

Before starting any task, ask this question in your mind – what do you want to do after completing your work? After asking this question, you will see your ability to work become stronger. Never regret the results of your decision. When you start prioritizing on yourself and continue on your chosen path, then you may lose opportunities in other spheres of life. Have faith in yourself. Keep greed and regret away from yourself. Do not waste time and focus on your work.

Represent people, share your experiences with them. Give importance to the people who are with you and give them full opportunity to present their abilities. Help them bring out their creativity. Do not interfere in their work. They just need more trust and support from you.

By organizing the time spent on different tasks and by carefully arranging them in order of priority increases your efficiency and productivity.

We can increase our ability to work provided we take proper care of our time. Do not destroy it. Plan to work according to this. If you waste time, stress increases, problems arise and your focus deviates from the goal. With this, your productivity also decreases.

Remember

- Time wastes him who wastes time. Therefore, use time properly.
- People say that no one receives before time and more than he is destined to. But you should walk in step with time.
- Difficult tasks take a little more time. So, trust yourself and be determined to do it with a plan.
- Use the time properly and take advantage of the opportunity. Then you can become a winner.
- Your brain can only have one thought at a time, which can be positive as well as negative. But you can turn negative thinking into positive thinking because you can do everything.
- Use time management tools, such as mobile, calendar or charts, etc., with the help of which tasks can be dealt with on timc. The habit of carelessness has to be abandoned.
- Do not waste time waiting for opportunities. Trust yourself and do your work.
- If you keep your clothes ready at night, then the time will not be wasted in the morning.
- Make a list while shopping. Most of our time is wasted in such tasks. So, make a list and get all the things at once.

Do Everything on Time

The student should decide his/her priorities, how much time he/she has to devote to studies and other tasks. Decide which subject has to be given priority, in which subject you are weak and which needs more attention.

Solve each other's problems in the group. Resolve the doubts of others. Get into the habit of learning in a group. Many times, students suffer from depression due to lack of confidence, which affects the study. Therefore, one should have confidence.

When filmmaker V. Shantaram suffered from an eye ailment, doctors tied a bandage over his eyes for three months. He used this free time to weave the story for 'Navrang' movie. As soon as he recovered, he immediately started with the production of the film. History is witness that it proved to be an unparalleled movie of its time, which broke all the box office records.

There are some reasons for lack of time where we ourselves are the centre and are unable to complete our work within the stipulated time frame. For example:

- We do not concentrate completely and do the work half-heartedly.
- Constantly recalling something to remember it.
- Not being alert.
- Lack of flexibility in working.
- Excessive length of rest period which causes unnecessary delay in starting another task after completion of the first task.
- Lack of information required for finishing the specified work.
- Inability to assess physical ability and maintain it in its present state.
- Falling sick again and again due to overwork.
- Having with many types of fear.
- Not executing work as planned.
- Not familiar with the technology required for the work.
- Laziness and postponing the task till the last moment.
- Becoming a soft target for some people.
- Quitting your work and start doing those tasks which are prescribed for someone else.
- Despite being aware of your busy schedule, taking up someone else's task out of inhibitions.
- Not being able to realistically assess the needs during the hours of the task.

- When planning time, do not consider the possible problems that may come up during the task.
- Not being able to plan for the use of the time between the two tasks.
- Unable to prioritize the tasks.

In this way we find that despite having enough time, we have to face time constraints. We cannot deny our responsibility in these matters. It is definitely possible for us to make up for the lack of time by improving our working style.

Many times, we are busy with work. But despite working all day, while leaving the office, we feel that our planned tasks have not been done today. There are no obvious reasons for the non-completion of tasks. But there are some indirect reasons, which lead to waste of productive time. For example:

- Not finding important things at their fixed place.
- Keeping the necessary papers or documents in a disorganized manner.
- Poor maintenance of files.
- Start work without thinking and planning.
- Unnecessary office decoration to attract your colleagues.
- If we do not decide the timeline for the task then it might take one, two days or weeks to do the work which can be done in one hour. If we set the time limit, the extra time that we are left with can be used for other things.
- Increase the efficiency of productive activities and the time taken for them by ten percent and decrease the time taken for non-essential activities by ten percent.
- Do not postpone any good work till tomorrow.
- Always keep your focus.
- Use appropriate technology. Focus on special skills and technologies that save time.
- Avoid unnecessary stress and habit of postponing work.

- Finish the day's work on the same day. When you work long hours, then the next day you will automatically start thinking of a better way of time management.
- Making the office staff wait unnecessarily.
- Attending a meeting without the necessary preparation.
- Organizing meetings without making necessary preparations on time.
- Unnecessarily prolonging the meeting.
- Paying too much attention to useless things.

The time which becomes unproductive due to such reasons can be definitely saved by careful planning.

- Divide your day into small parts as required, set the task for each part and place it on the table. If the priority needs to be changed according to the demands of the circumstances, then change them. But do it by writing it down.
- Most of the tasks are of repetitive nature. Make a list of such tasks, make preparations beforehand and keep it. Starting anew every time consumes a lot of time. Think about the tasks that have to be repeated and how they can be done easily.
- We need to motivate those causing interruptions to work. Explain the benefits of working. Tell them that if we do not do our work honestly, how will we be able to motivate the children in our family? If children are not encouraged by our work, how will they become useful in future?
- Understand the importance of multi-tasking. Can anything be done while waiting in a waiting line, watching television, walking, cleaning? Always keep a pocket diary and a pen with you so that good ideas can be written down immediately.
- Introduce commitment during work, and stay away from everything that distracts you.
- Find out your bad habit that consumes time, and work towards getting rid of it.

- The problem of not remembering the things that are needed for work leads to unnecessary wastage of time. For this, the habit of writing down can prove beneficial. It is better to keep a pocket diary with you. The diary proves to be an effective way to make time valuable and to prevent the unnecessary overloading of the mind.

It is natural for interruptions to occur during work. But we should think about the reasons and factors which are within our control and also those which are not in our power. It is true that we can shrewdly and smartly avoid most of the interruptions that occur during the course of work. If someone approaches us aimlessly, then still remaining busy and without leaving our work, we can raise our head and smile and continue doing our work.

- The work becomes dull when you do the same thing. Try swapping tasks.
- 'I am not in the mood right now; I will do it later.' 'There is still a lot of time.' Set aside these excuses and start the work you have set out to do.
- Efficient people finish the task in one day which others take a week to finish. If you want to be the most productive person, then bid adieu to inertia, laziness, habit of wasting time and lethargy so that work can be done before the deadline.
- Our motivation is to get rid of boredom. Therefore, do each task with all your heart. Most people are not very productive not because they do not know the job, rather they do not want to work.
- Never make the average person or colleague your role model.
- Learn to love the work you do.
- Do the work at hand with full diligence. At that time, take special care that there are no distractions.
- It is important to save time in time management. Repeated mistakes are a huge waste of time. Regular practice is necessary to avoid this. A great musician has said that if I

do not practise for a day, then I know immediately; if I do not do it for two days, my wife gets to know it and if I do not practise for three days, then the audience gets to know.

- Discard fear of adopting new ideas and technology. It feels like spending a lot of time in the beginning. But in future, it can save time beyond imagination.
- Before starting your work, make sure that all the things that you may need are available with you. Those who work without interruption save about 20 percent of their time.
- To stay fresh, work for success in life as well as meaningfulness.
- To get a rebate of 25 rupees, it is not wise to go 15 kilometres and buy that item. It is nothing but wasting time.
- Reserve that part of the day when you feel most refreshed. During that time, perform serious tasks that demand excessive thinking and analysis.
- Get up half an hour early in the morning and add 15 to 30 hours in a month.
- If you stop learning, then there will be laziness. Laziness is a major obstacle in time management. Always keep your level of enthusiasm and interest high with respect to learning.
- Study as if you have to teach the subject to someone. Better understanding saves a lot of time.
- Make a habit of keeping things in certain places. Negligence causes wastage of time. Remember, many times you have to spend hours searching for the keys of house or car.
- The name of the file or folder should be based on your general thinking so that unnecessary time is not spent. It is better to make a habit of writing the file name with your document while working on the computer. Time that is spent in searching again and again will be saved.
- Take the right action and also immediately with the necessary guidelines. By doing this, the work will be quick and good quality.

- If the work pressure is low at any time, then use it appropriately for your skill development. At this time, avoid daydreaming and do your analysis.
- To keep yourself and your office organized, keep a scope for it in your plan so that important tasks can be dealt with as necessary.
- While keeping in mind possible interruptions and fatigue during work, also remember to take the time for rest, entertainment, etc. during time management.
- Always proceed with an option. Invite solutions along with problems so that better decisions can be taken in advance and you do not have to spend unnecessary time in changing the decision.

If we are committed to time management, then we will feel the need to change the way we do our work many areas. But do not forget that it is not easy to bring any kind of positive change. As long as we do not want it with our heart and stick to our resolve, the matter is not resolved.

That is why we have to think how to use our time, that is, how we will achieve our short-term and long-term goals. We alone have to think how to plan and allocate time keeping in mind our set goals. In order to use our time judiciously and rationally, we have to make a distinction between the important and the urgent and the task list has to be prepared according to priority keeping the time in mind.

❑

Diving into the Infinite Ocean of Knowledge

"The scholar is praised by all people. He is worshipped everywhere. All kinds of benefits are gained from learning. Knowledge is worshipped everywhere. Therefore, acquire as much knowledge as possible."

–Chanakya

A student whose mind gets attracted to embellishments or grooming spends most of his time in these things and is deprived of diving into the infinite ocean of knowledge.

Such people keep working hard to show themselves to be most beautiful and different at all times and for this reason, their minds are always occupied with matters related to beauty, good attire and lifestyle. The grooming is not limited to this. It progresses further to cause the distinction and attraction between men and women. A person who thinks about grooming is never able to attain knowledge by focusing in one place. A student should avoid such situations.

Students whose minds are preoccupied with grooming are not able to concentrate on their studies. Matters related to beauty, attire and lifestyle keep going on in their minds and later on they experience failure.

Therefore, Chanakya further says that do not love the body much. It is necessary for the body to be healthy. We will be able to work hard only when there is energy in the body. But students who only pay attention to the beauty and body every moment turn away from education. Attention should be paid to study more than the body.

People who spend a lot of time looking after their body constantly move farther from studies and education. They focus only on physical beauty and their interest in studies starts to diminish. Even while studying, they keep thinking about what is lacking in their body today, due to which their concentration is affected. This results in their failure in achieving the goals. The person who pays more attention to his body gets distressed by a small wound or pain. He accepts defeat even before facing great difficulties.

Also, Acharya Chanakya believes that excessive entertainment can be harmful for students. Entertainment should be sought only as much as it is necessary. Excessive entertainment causes decline in the youth's power.

They say that the process of learning is endless and eternal which continuously undergoes changes. The complete knowledge puts an end to doubts and leads to closing of arguments. Completeness of knowledge is always a goal. As soon as the veil is removed from one mystery, the other mystery poses a challenge. This sequence of events remains constant. In practice, it is said that where there is knowledge, there is no place for doubts. But the reality is that where there are doubts, there is an open flow of knowledge. Even if one finds it strange, but the truth is that our doubts carry forward our journey for knowledge and motivate us to continue growing.

According to Chanakya, knowledge is so multidimensional that a human being is able to talk about one aspect of an object or idea at a time. Our doubts about an object or idea indicate that the desire to know that object has been born within us. When we question why the Earth revolves around the Sun, we certainly get a sense of the earlier question that the Earth revolves around the Sun. Why does the Earth revolve around the Sun? What is its speed and reason? Where does the energy come from? How is it related to the motion of other planets, satellites? The endless series of such questions begins with a single question. It is not necessary that all the questions should come to mind of a person at once. But during mutual discussion, debates, contemplation or different times in history, these questions keep arising.

It can be said that the questions are seeds. One sprinkle is followed by a spate of questions. Our unanswered questions tell us that knowing is just a stop. There is also a limit to the equipment used in the pursuit of knowledge. Despite this, at any given stage of knowledge, we get connected to a long series of questions about it. In the ongoing process of learning, we get answers to some question while some remain unanswered. Similarly, knowledge progresses in the first and secondary stages. This tradition is so long and extensive that our level of knowledge is always at the first stage. As curious people, we always find ourselves faced with a new goal, which always remains the target.

Learning Process

Since childhood, the child is told about the various objects around him and their designs. These designs exist in the form of individual images in our brain. During the process of learning, a person learns what an object is by comparing a particular object or idea with the images present in the brain. It is not necessary that all the designs are present in the mind of every individual. In that situation, the person manages with the experiences and images that the others have. In this way, knowledge is also a collective process.

Man accumulated different experiences while wandering through different areas on the earth. As a result, different languages took birth. On the basis of interaction with the civilizations, the period of linguistic change promotion also continued. One can say that knowledge is intellectual-experiential wealth acquired by the association with the nature. Only man has received the gift of memory from nature. Through this, he has been passing on his experiences, knowledge, etc. to the future generations. Hundreds of generations have contributed to the enlightenment of today's man. Humans have prepared the criteria of what we call knowledge. These criteria have also been amended from time to time.

Knowledge is infinite. Like other activities of the society, both the journey of knowledge and its evaluation are relative to time. The level of knowledge indicates the state of rationalization of man and his society. The characteristic of knowledge is that it exists but it does not have a shape. The intellectuals have been doing the work of designing knowledge. Since even the greatest intellectuals have limitations, an individual is able to gather only a part of the vast wealth of knowledge. On the basis of that, he evaluates social events and individuals. It is like a measuring the earth with a small coin. Since time immemorial, there has been an attempt to control knowledge, to adapt it, to make it work whichever way we want. History is not free from presumptions. Hence sociocultural scholars consider historical facts as incomplete, one sided and concocted.

Better Results in Studies

Keeping awake whole nights to study or rote learning are not a guarantee of good marks in the exam. According to Chanakya, better performance in examinations depends not only on how much you have studied, but more importantly on your method of studying. Even after studying continuously for several hours, you may not get better results than your friend who gets the same result with a less but well-planned study.

Actually, keeping awake whole nights to study or rote learning are not a guarantee of good marks in the exam. It depends on the smart habits that you use for studying. In reality, studying in a planned and focused manner also broadens your understanding while improving your results.

In today's competitive era, studying and passing with good marks is no less than winning a war and to win this war, one needs to strategize and prepare accordingly. Usually, due to the lack of proper guidance, students are not able to prepare properly and as the time of examination draws near, they start growing nervous and anxious.

Get rid of the habit of postponing work: To be successful, you will have to give up the habit of postponing tasks. Do the work that is necessary at the right time. Kaal kare so aaj kar, aaj kare so ab; that is, we should do the work of tomorrow today itself and we should do today's work now.

Suitable place of study: It is very important to choose a suitable and quiet place to study. The place of study should be such that you can sit and read with full concentration and calm mind. If the house is small or there is no such suitable place in the house, then it would be better to go to a quiet place outside the house, go to a friend's house or a library.

Time-table for studies: To be successful, it is necessary to follow the schedule prescribed for studies. Allocate a certain time for each subject in the time-table. Only by making a correct time-table, you will be able to give proper attention to every subject. And it is not enough just to make a time-table, it is also necessary to strictly follow it.

Sports and recreation: Along with studies, sports and recreation are also necessary for the all-round development of the student. Sports leads to physical and mental development, and entertainment lightens the mood.

Dividing big task in small parts: If the task is big, divide it into small parts. This makes that task easier. Similarly, in studies too, big lessons can be made easier by dividing them into smaller parts. This makes studying easy and interesting.

Know your energy level: Every person's physical and mental energy level can be different at different times of the day. For example, some people feel fresher and more energetic in the morning whereas some people feel fresher and more energetic in the evening or at night. Some people remember when they study in the morning and some remember when they study late at the night. So, the time when you feel fresher and more energetic is the time that is favourable for your studies.

Rest between studies: Your mind gets tired while studying. Whenever you feel tired, take a short rest. Generally, one should take a little rest after an hour while studying.

Highlight the main points: Always keep a highlighter with you whenever you sit down to study. If you see anything important, then highlight it immediately. This will help you a lot during revision.

Set a goal: Set a goal as to which lesson or book you want to complete in certain number of days, which topic needs special attention or what percentage of marks will be required to go to your favourite college. In this way, it is very important to set goals for your studies. If you study setting the goal for the week and month, then at the end of the year you will be able to prepare for the exam properly without panicking.

Use all the senses: While studying, use your five sense organs – eyes, nose, ears, tongue and skin as much as possible. Look carefully at the pictures and charts, etc. printed in the book. If possible, experiment in the laboratory or look at the model related to the subject.

Use of intelligence boosting techniques: If you know about intelligent boosting techniques or you have learnt them from somewhere, then use them in your studies. These techniques are very scientific and effective.

Balanced food: Eat a balanced home cooked meal. Avoid foreign traditional food and drinks. Eat heavy breakfast in the morning. Lunch should be light and dinner should be lighter than that. If possible, eat only fruit, salad and soup etc. for dinner.

Stay healthy: A healthy mind resides in a healthy body. So, go for a walk in the morning and exercise according to your ability. The healthier your body is, the more active and confident you will be.

Curiosity Solution: If you have any question in your mind or you do not understand the answer to any question, then feel free to ask for help from your teacher. Teachers like the student who really wants to learn and are always ready to help him.

Use of resources: Make full use of all the resources available for studies. Read the books carefully. Go to the library. Seek help from your teachers and parents. Ask for help from friends and elder siblings. Make positive use of all the available resources like internet-television, etc.

Self-encouragement: Encourage yourself before going to the examination hall. Recall the events of your life when you were successful. Believe that you have been successful during difficult situations and examinations in the past. You will also pass this exam with good marks. Such positive thoughts boost morale and lead to better performance in the exam.

Message of Acharya Chanakya

Acharya Chanakya has given an identical message for the seven kinds of people – students, servants, passers-by, hungry people, those who are stricken with fear, storekeeper and gatekeeper should be awakened if they are asleep because their duty is to fulfil their job responsibility and not sleeping.

When these seven kinds of people sleep, it indicates neglect and is harmful. So, when you wake them up, there will be gratitude.

If the student sleeps, he will lag behind in learning; if the passer-by sleeps, he will be robbed; hungry and scared people do not generally sleep; but if they are sleeping, then you should wake them up. Similarly, if the storekeeper and guard sleep, it is likely to cause harm. So, they should not be allowed to sleep at the wrong time.

A king, a child, a dog belonging to someone else, a foolish man, a snake, a tiger and a pig – these seven should never be awakened from sleep. Awakening them will only cause harm and there will be no benefit. It will be difficult for you to protect yourself from their attack. So, it is better for you to walk ahead when you see them sleeping.

One does not get wealth if a spiritless and ineffectual person is happy nor does one feel fearful if he gets upset. One does not worry about upsetting a person if one does not get any award due to his grace nor is he entitled to punish anyone.

The point is that if the person can't harm you, why should you care about him?

Succeeding in a Competitive Era

In today's competitive era, every person wants to come first, every person wants to succeed although the definition of success can be different for everyone. Whenever we have small successes, our confidence increases. But when we face a defeat, we get discouraged. We need to understand that life is like an ECG graph. Till the ECG graph keeps moving up and down, our heart keeps working. But when a straight line appears, the heart stops working and life ends. Similarly, if there are no ups and downs in life, it becomes uninteresting. Therefore, facing failures in life is as important as having successes. When man experiences success after facing failures, only then he can enjoy the success to its fullest.

The biggest mistake you can make in life is being afraid of making a mistake. Do not be afraid of failing, nor waste your energy trying to hide your failure. If you are not failing then you are not developing. When successful people stop developing and learning, it is because they have lost the desire to take the risk of failure. Failure is not defeat; it is merely a delay. It is not a closed road, but it is a temporarily winding road to reach success.

Everybody makes mistakes, especially those who take risks. Failure is often the first necessary step to success. If we do not take the risk of failure then we will not get the chance to succeed. If we are trying, it means that we are winning. Failing is a natural result of trying. Never let the fear of failing become a barrier in the way of victory.

Sometimes defeat is just a ladder of victory. Henry Ford had said that a mistake may also prove to be necessary for significant achievement in future. Some learn from their mistakes and some never recover from them. Learn how to fail intelligently and develop success in failure.

Frustration and failure are the two most credible steps of success. If a person studies them and wants to take full advantage of them, then he will benefit from them more than anything else. Most people consider success and failure to be antithetical, but in reality, these two are the result of the same process.

The season of failure is the best time to sow the seeds of success. Successful people are not afraid of failure. They suffer one failure after another until they succeed. If you want to increase the speed of your success, then the best way to do this is to double your failure rate. The law of failure is one of the most powerful rules of success.

In order to achieve success in life, it is very important that we do not let our mind suffer from the fear of failure. It becomes difficult for a person to succeed who has this fear that he will not be able to do anything in life. Therefore, it is very important that we abandon this kind of mindset from today and now.

❑

8

Habits, Discipline and Success

"We do not become inferior when we do not have wealth. One is certainly rich if he has knowledge. One who does not have the gem of knowledge is inferior to everything. His wealth is also meaningless."

–Chanakya

Acharya Chanakya says that even ordinary trees become fragrant like sandalwood when touched by the air coming from the Malayachala mountain. Only bamboo tree that is hollow is not affected by the wind. Likewise, wise advice has no effect on individuals or students who lack internal qualities. The point is that people should not be blamed for their lack of understanding because due to the lack of intellectual power, they cannot understand anything because the brain of such persons is like a hollow bamboo. Even the Vedas and scriptures cannot help a person who is unintelligent. This is just like a mirror is useless for a blind person because a mirror cannot bring light to his eyes.

It means that just as the great scriptures, Vedas, etc. have no meaning for a stupid person, in the same way, a mirror is also meaningless for a blind person. On the other hand, for a normal person, the above two things have their own importance. The person who has intelligence also has all kinds of strength. He overcomes all difficult situations with ease by facing them.

The power of a stupid person is also useless because he is unable to use it properly. Using the power of intellect, a small rabbit had killed a powerful lion by making him fall into a well. This was possible only with the strength of his intellect.

An elephant with such a heavy body is tamed with a small goad. Everyone knows that the goad is very small in size. The lighted lamp dissipates the surrounding darkness, while the darkness is much wider and extensive than the lamp. A thunderbolt breaks large mountains even though the thunderbolt is much smaller in size than the mountain. The point is that controlling such a big elephant with a goad, breaking huge and enormous mountains with a small thunderbolt, the elimination of dense darkness with a small lit lamp are evidences of the fact that only the brightest light triumphs. There is power only in the radiance. It is useless to consider obese and tall people as strong.

Acharya Chanakya says that it is a harsh truth that even after reasoning in different ways, a wicked man does not turn into a good man just like a neem tree watered with ghee and milk does not become sweet. Just as the neem tree watered with ghee and milk does not become sweet, reason with the evil man in any way, he cannot give up his wickedness. Therefore, it is futile to try to persuade and reform an evil man.

It is Important to Change the Habits

According to Chanakya, habits are an integral part of a human being's life. Some of these habits raise the human being to the higher class and some destroy his life. Our habits make or break us. Good habits lead us to good discipline and success. Therefore, to make children smart, it is necessary to inculcate right qualities in children since childhood.

Often children study only when it becomes absolutely necessary, otherwise they do not even touch books. So, the first task is to fix the study time. At this time, the child will study and make notes even if the examination is not close. This will instil in the child the desire to study, such as completing homework properly and submitting it on time, preparing before the exam time approaches and getting good marks by working hard. Teach children to make notes – this will make them understand more and it will be easier for them to revise it further. Making notes will also make the preparation for the exam comfortable.

It is necessary to create the right environment for the children to study and one of the parents will have to be with them. You can do some of your work, read a book and make children sit next to you to study. Turn off the TV and everyone can keep doing their work with full focus. Believe me, children's focus on study will increase. The more you stay connected with children at the time of their study, the better the children will do. No matter how many tuition classes you make them attend, send them to coaching classes, make a good study room – all this will not work as much as your involvement with the child with dedication will work. Spend time together, keep track of your child's progress, and always be close and show them the right path to help them solve their problems. This will be enough to make the child focus on study.

Any work done continuously throughout the month becomes a habit. Instil the habit of studying slowly. See improvement by inculcating a new habit and then advising the child further. Together these good habits will succeed in helping them triumph in life.

It is not a good habit to postpone your work. Until you finish your work, you will live under constant tension. It is good to change the habit of avoiding work and living a stress-free life. Many people have this habit of pulling other people's legs frequently. Sometimes this habit may cause you to lose a good friendship and sometimes the other person may pull your leg if they get a chance.

Do not believe other people too soon nor get trapped in their advice and make a thoughtless decision. Take advice, but do think it over. When the child returns from school, please check his copy or diary. Whatever has been taught in the school, discuss it with the child. If the mother is busy with the household chores, then the father should fulfil this responsibility.

Change the habit of flattery, too because those who flatter are mocked behind their backs. Do not try to get close to someone to fulfil your selfish motives. Never resort to lies to move forward. You have to face embarrassment when you are caught lying and it also has far-reaching effects.

Do not depend on others for your work, nor expect much from others. If expectations are not met, you feel disappointed. Do as much as you can on your own. Never speak ill of others in front of children. Children are small, but they understand everything. Instil the habit of greeting the elders in children. Do not hesitate while talking to someone. Explain yourself gently. Do not impose your orders or wishes.

Whenever you speak, speak thoughtfully immaterial of whether the other person in front of you is small or big. Always keep the same routine for children. Even on holidays or Sundays, make it a habit to wake them early in the morning. Most parents allow children to sleep late on holidays which is a wrong habit.

Time is very powerful. Know its importance and try to achieve your objectives by not wasting time. Maintain the friendliest behaviour. Do not have conflicts when dealing with people. Cordiality in relationships keeps them alive and thriving. Go to school on time. Do not take leave without any particular reason. Inform the teacher on time when it is really needed.

Do not waste time in criticizing other. Criticism can also sometimes cause quarrels. Concentrate, study or do other things, do not waste your attention in useless things. Teach children the importance of money. Do not buy them anything immediately. Tell them that they can have anything if they study. With this, the child will learn about the importance of education, hard work and money from childhood.

Ideal Student

According to Chanakya, the ideal student is the foundation of the nation. The honour, prestige and pride of the country are based on them. The progress and decline of the nation rests on them. A nation whose students are well-educated and disciplined are a source of inspiration for that country or for society. There is an old saying:

Kak cheshta, vako dhyanam, shwan nidra tathaiv ch|

Alphari, griha tyagi, vidyarthi panch lakshanam||

Kak Chesta

(Behaviour like a crow – clever)

Vako dhyanam

(Meditating like heron)

Shwan nidra tathaiv cha

(Sleep like a dog who wakes up instantly)

Alpahari

(Less indulgent, eating less food)

Gruh tyagi

(One who leaves the house)

Vidyarthi panch lakshanam

(These are the five characteristics of a true and good student.)

The ideal student should always keep his eyes on his goal, on his destination. This is the distinguishing quality of an ideal student. Students should always keep their focus on teacher and study-related activities while receiving education. Just as a heron keeps its focus only on hunting by standing in water, a student should always focus on his purpose.

Alert sleep is a special quality of an ideal student. He should always be alert in his sleep. Sleeping early and waking up early makes a person healthy, wealthy and intelligent. The ideal student should sleep at ten o'clock at night and wake up at four o'clock in the morning.

The diet of the ideal student should be less because on eating more, he becomes sleepy and lethargic and lethargy is the enemy of an ideal student. He should be prompt about his work.

It is necessary for the ideal student to leave his home, because the ideal student is like a garden. Just as a garden spreads its fragrance in the world, a student with his virtues and qualities affects the society, the nation and the whole world.

An ideal student should obey the instructions of parents and teachers, respect elders, follow the rules and discipline, be virtuous, be friendly with peers, stay away from bad company, inspire the younger people to follow the path, be patient, be polite and gentle. He should absorb only the good qualities like a swan.

Avoid Bad Feelings

A person who has bad feelings in his mind remains disturbed all the time. Such a person can adopt any path, right or wrong, for the fulfilment of his desires. If a student falls in the wrong company, he gives up study and gets attracted towards other things. All his attention is focused only on fulfilling his evil demands and he grows distant from education. Therefore, students should avoid such feelings.

Do not Waste Time in Fooling Around

The most important quality of a good student is seriousness. It is very important for the student to adopt this quality in order to receive education and get success in life. A student who wastes all his time in fooling around is never successful. It is very important to have a stable mind in order to absorb knowledge and a student who fools around is never able to keep his mind stable.

Avoid Excessive Sleep

6 to 8 hours of sleep is sufficient for a healthy human being. Students should make sure that they avoid excessive sleep. Excessive sleep always leads to physical fatigue and it becomes difficult for one to concentrate when the body is tired, whereas it is very important to concentrate your mind on study.

❑

9 Quenching your Curiosity

"Knowledge written in books and money deposited with others never works on time. Such knowledge or wealth should be understood as non-existent."

–Chanakya

Chanakya was a diplomat and eminent economist. He established Chandragupta as a ruler on the basis of the strength of his knowledge and intelligence and gave a new turn to the history. He has documented his knowledge and experience in books like Economics, Ethics, etc. Chanakya says that a civilized person is the one who has dignity and consideration. Chanakya has talked about the man living with civilization. But according to Chanakya, the person should not hesitate while performing some tasks, otherwise he may suffer due to these things in life.

According to Acharya Chanakya, there should never be any shame in learning any skill. One should not hesitate or be shy while learning. A person should be unashamed while learning and satiate his curiosity. A person who is hesitant to learn does not get full knowledge, and he is left behind in life due to lack of education.

Introspect

No person is born great in life. He becomes great by his actions, by his principles. Human being is an effigy of mistakes. But the person who introspects and corrects his mistakes and does not repeat them wins every race of life.

Every morning we get up to do our daily chores and go to bed every evening and sleep. After all, how much time do we spend on ourselves? If you ask this question to yourself, the answer will be 'Absolutely none'.

It is very easy for us to speak ill of others and their shortcomings because we enjoy criticizing others so much that we are not aware of the hours gone by. But have you ever introspected? If you look within yourself, you will find that you too have many shortcomings and flaws, which you have never tried to find out or have ignored and disregarded them.

By introspecting, you not only discover your shortcomings, you also get a good chance to overcome them. Remember, no person is virtuous. But efforts can be made to become a good and virtuous human being. These values embodied in life since childhood make a person a great human being and give superior citizens to the community.

Student and Teacher Relationship

Acharya Chanakya says that student life is a time to polish oneself. If gold is not heated in the fire, how will it become pure? Similarly in life, the harder the students work, the more they will advance on the path of progress. And teachers also have a big role in the progress of students.

According to Acharya Chanakya, teacher has a very important role in a student's life. The interaction of student and teacher is of great importance during the long student life of early days. If at this time, teachers pay profound attention towards building the lives of children, then there is no doubt that out of these children, great men, scholars, ascetics, public servants, public leaders, skilled leaders will emerge. The burden of our country, society, civilization, culture rests on the shoulders of teachers. Realizing this responsibility, more efforts are necessary for building excellent personality in children. It is a big responsibility for teachers today.

In India, since ancient times, the relationship between Guru and disciple is based on faith, reverence and trust. Along with formal education, one also needs to learn in practical life. The education we receive in school is our formal education. But on many occasions even in personal life, some people keep guiding us in the form of a teacher through various practical aspects of life including work, behaviour, spiritual life etc. Our relationship with our teacher in any aspect of life is always based on rights and duties, which are complementary to each other. The rights and duties in the society should be complied with in a good spirit and create an environment in which all teachers can become the bearers of education and knowledge dissemination in the society.

In the scriptures, the mother, father and teacher are considered to be important in building the life of a child. Parents raise and nurture the child and the teachers develop his intellectual, spiritual qualities and character. They teach him about life and the world and awaken his consciousness. Therefore, the teacher has been given an important place in our culture and is revered. From the teachings of the guru, his behaviour and his character, the child learns how to live life. This is why teachers have been given great respect and prestige in our society.

The student learns a lot from the teacher's work, philosophy, etc. The student will try to emulate the same philosophy in his life as that of the teacher's. For this reason, the teacher has been asked to be optimistic. The attitude of the teacher towards education will be reflected by his students. Faith encourages learning. Therefore, he should have complete devotion towards both his teaching and the subject. If he does not do this, then he will not be able to develop the personality of his students which is the main goal of education.

A student should study with enthusiasm and readiness. By doing this, he can generate affection towards learning. It is also absolutely necessary for students to have a scientific outlook because they are the future citizens who will later bear the burden of establishing the country and society. If the scientific attitude is not developed in the students, then they will be unable to lead a successful social life and will not be able to overcome the struggles, disadvantages and discord in the society.

Along with this, it is also mandatory for the student to have a liberal attitude. From this point of view, he can develop qualities like humility, sympathy, love etc. If he lacks this attitude, then he will be unable to work for the welfare of human society and will not be able to generate a sense of cosmopolitanism. Therefore, it is very important for students to have a liberal attitude.

The student should be an ideal citizen. He should have the qualities of an ideal citizen and should behave according to them. He should have full knowledge of the duties and rights of a citizen. Along with this, he should present an ideal before the society by behaving according to them, view the rights of other people with respect and work in the society with cooperation, collaboration, love, honesty and enthusiasm. In a society consisting of castes, sub-castes and classes, it is necessary to have the qualities of tolerance, patience, sympathy, generosity and kindness towards human beings, democratic approach etc.

It is necessary for the student to be socially active. He should serve the society. For this, he should participate actively in social work at the local and regional level and try to be successful in assuming leadership. He should participate fully in social work and policy making work and should present an ideal by presenting qualities of cooperation, collaboration, justice, sympathy etc. in front of the society.

The personality of the student is the cornerstone of a successful society. It is essential to for a student to inculcate these qualities in his personality – vitality, good health, truthfulness, well-wisher, optimism, fairness, patience, inventiveness, cooperation, tolerance, love, self-control, large heartedness, warm-heartedness, readiness, enthusiasm, loyalty etc.

Students are an important part of the educational process. Without students, the process of education cannot run successfully. The process and conduct of education also have an impact on other students, school and society. From this point of view, it is said that students are nation builders.

A class has different types of students, they have different problems. In order for them to learn well, their problems have to be resolved. A teacher can only solve the problems of students if he is familiar with them. To know about their problems, the teacher should have knowledge of psychology. Only with the knowledge of psychology, the teacher can understand the interest, aptitude, ability, intelligence, etc. of the student and on the basis of that, he can successfully carry out the process of his teaching. A good student is the one who always has the urge to learn. In other words, we can say that a good student is the one who always remains the student. An important quality of a good student is his punctuality. He should attend the school on time, attend the prayer meeting and leave the school on time at the end of the day.

It is also necessary for a smart student to be effective. According to Chanakya, a student's personality can be effective only if it has the following qualities:

Attire

A smart student should wear a clean, ironed uniform to make his personality impressive. Hair should be combed properly when he arrives in the class. This makes a good impression on other students.

Good Health

It is also necessary for a smart student to be physically healthy. If the student is not healthy then how will he study in the class and how will he learn? When he is physically unfit, he will remain unfit mentally. Therefore, it is necessary for the smart students to be physically and mentally healthy.

Strong Character

A smart student should have a strong character. His character also affects other students. Therefore, a smart student should present himself well in front of his fellow students. Never commit any wrong or immoral act in front of them.

Leadership Power

A smart student should also have leadership power. He should provide efficient and effective leadership to his fellow students in every field, course-related process, discussion on any subject, maintaining discipline, etc. so that they can work successfully in all these areas.

Patience

It is necessary for a smart student to have the quality of patience. He should not lose patience over small matters, rather he should answer questions carefully with patience.

Enthusiasm

A smart student is enthusiastic. Whatever task is given to him, he carries it out with full enthusiasm. This also generates interest in his fellow students and they also cooperate with full enthusiasm, which increases the chances of getting complete success in the work.

Self-respect

It is necessary for a smart student to have a sense of self-respect. A smart student never succumbs to wrong things in front of teachers, headmaster and others. He does not tolerate any kind of injustice. He does not compromise for the wrong things. Smart students who are conscious of their duties and rights are able to guard their self-esteem.

The task of a smart student is not just to go to class and read books. He should also see how much influence he has on his fellow students. He can see this only when a good relationship is established with his fellow students. For this, he should pay personal attention to each student, solve their problems appropriately and be friendly with them.

Students should also build good relations with the community where the school is located. With this, the individuals in the community can prove to be helpful in the progress of the school. Students can seek the support of teachers with a view to building relationships with the community.

Cheerfulness

If you are in a joyful environment then your body and mind work in the best manner. If you live without a single moment of agitation, irritability, anxiety, restlessness or anger, and stay comfortably happy then it is said that your ability to use intelligence can increase by 100% in a single day. Your happy existence makes you capable of having a higher sense of perception and more capable for functioning. Unless you are happy, you cannot inspire anyone else to be happy. If we are happy, then whatever we do, whatever we make, whatever we create, we will see this quality in it.

Whether one is a student or a businessman, whether one is running a country or it is any other task in the world, when we become too goal-focused, the end result and not life becomes important. Whatever work we do, whatever the outcome of it, our focus should be on how to do that work in the most beautiful way with honesty and truth. Till now we have just kept thinking about educating children. The most important thing is that teachers should constantly develop and keep improving. Excitement and enthusiasm in children are such that you need ten people's energy to handle them.

It should be made a rule in the country that every parent should attend their child's school at least thrice a year and must spend at least one day in school. They must know what kind of education is being imparted in the school, how it is being imparted and what their children are doing. It is necessary to create a culture of participation of the parents in their children's education. No beautiful and good thing can ever happen without participation. Education system should not be like a machinery through which our children come out. Till now we have just been thinking about educating children. The most important thing is that teachers should constantly develop and keep growing. This development should not happen in them with respect to their ability to teach, but also with respect to their development as human beings.

It is not just about teaching a subject. Rather it is about being fully engrossed in the process of teaching, entrepreneurial approach and full of newness. Only a teacher who inspires can make education beautiful. This determines whether the students are enjoying their studies or not.

People spend many years of their lives in educational institutions. It is a place where everything gets moulded and is given shape. Therefore, it is important that they should be good. The kind of education system we have today is largely reminiscent of the colonial era. We have made minor changes in that education system, but we have not really restructured it.

It is important for the teacher to know what his students think, how they think, and how they can be helped. Children grow up emulating the society and culture. Society and culture determine the nature of their learning. To a large extent, this nature determines what the child will learn and how he will learn, or which things will be easy for him to learn and which things will be difficult to learn. These matters are of importance for a teacher. There are often two types of children in our schools. One - who are well prepared for the school and the school environment. That means that there are educated people in their homes, who are able to teach such things to their children that are part of the school culture. But on the other hand, there are children who are deprived of these facilities and are not closely acquainted with the school and its culture. They find a lot of things to be unfamiliar in the school. In such a situation, it is beneficial for the child to have a close relationship with the teacher and talk to them at different levels, which also gives the teacher an opportunity to understand the child. It is the responsibility of the teachers to provide right education, motivation, tolerance, behavioural change and guidance to their children to make their future bright. Teachers can lay the foundation for establishing a positive relationship by getting to know each of their students better.

❑

10 Staying Focused on the Goal

"Do not reveal your plan about what you have thought of doing. It is good to keep it a secret and be determined to work on it until it is successful."

–Chanakya

According to Chanakya, before performing any task, find out your goal. Getting education with a goal in life develops the talent of the student. Every student should choose his/her goal keeping the society in mind. Some people set a big goal for themselves. They keep their attention focused on it at all times and even abandon all their comforts to achieve it. Many of them also become successful. They feel satisfied after achieving their goals. But it is one of the ways of living.

There are many people whose goals are not far-reaching. Even if they have such goals, they are not serious about them.

They set small objectives and do not struggle much for them. If they achieve it, it's fine and if they don't, they have no remorse. We cannot call the lives of such people meaningless because there is a pleasure even in making efforts. It is possible that a person who gives importance to small pleasures has touched different dimensions of life more than a person who ignores immediate experiences for a greater cause. Therefore, a man with a small aim often achieves more than his set goal.

The element that is required to achieve success is having a goal.

Any person in this world who is successful does something for this world in some form or the other. To achieve success in life, one must set one's own goals. People without any aim are a burden on this earth. They only exist, they do not live. Their goal is to eat and drink, that is, their aim is to just spend their lives.

On the contrary, the person who sets a goal in his life achieves success. Also, they give something to this world. For example, suppose a person is a teacher, then he is not a teacher working for his own livelihood alone. He is sharing his knowledge with others. He is telling other people how to live since they have got this life. Those who want to achieve success, they receive education for that. On the other hand, there are aimless people who do not receive education. This means that a teacher is doing his duty and giving something to this world in form of his knowledge, but there are some people who do not want to receive that knowledge.

If you look around, you will see many aimless people. I have a neighbour. Whenever I ask him – "Friend, what's going on?" He has only one answer – "Thirty have passed, twenty are left. They too shall pass".

He has no goal in life. His goal is to only 'pass time', which means that he is merely living his life. When a goal is set, it is natural that there will be some obstacles in achieving it. But the one who overcomes these obstacles succeeds.

Therefore, when a goal is set, it is important to achieve it. Obstacles keep coming, but do not be distracted by them. A person who is afraid of obstacles coming in the way can never achieve his goal. Just as the archer Arjuna saw only the bird's eye, in the same way to achieve success, one should keep his eyes focused only on his goal to achieve the goal he had set. Those who are jealous of your success can become the obstacles and they can confuse you.

There is a goal hidden behind every task. If a person is sitting somewhere or standing somewhere, he has no goal. But if he gets up from that place or moves from the place where he is standing, then he is doing it for a goal, to do something. If someone did a good deed, set a target, beat someone and killed him, then it can be said that he did it for a goal. That is, no work takes place without a goal.

Setting a goal does not mean that you have set it and your job is over. After setting a goal, many obstacles can arise in the process of achieving it. Achieving your goal by crossing those hurdles is success. It is certain that there will be obstacles in the path of success. But it is self-confidence to cross them patiently without being afraid of them that leads man to the goal. When a child learns to walk, he falls several times. He then gets up and walks again. In this way, he learns to walk because he is confident of standing up and he succeeds.

When some people see others succeed, they try to distract them from their goals by discouraging them. But people who remain focused on their goals like the star of Dhruv become an inspiration for everyone.

The goal achieved with the help of someone else without any effort is a temporary success. The goal thus achieved can distract you from your work and may make you go astray. Then you will get into that habit. You will become dependent on others. Focus steadily on your goal. Set a definite goal in life and go ahead and achieve success.

❑

Challenges of Student Life

"After each drop of water, the pitcher is filled slowly. Similarly, all learning, religion and wealth accumulate gradually."

–Chanakya

Acharya Chanakya says that the usefulness of knowledge lies in living and conducting one's life in accordance. Life without knowledge is as meaningless as the existence of an army without a commander.

Chanakya was a teacher himself. That is why he says that the student life is the most beautiful and the most challenging phase. Students should be cautious at every step and use the time properly. Student life is a life of cultivation and penance. This period is of concentrated study and contemplation of knowledge.

This is the time to keep yourself away from worldly distractions. For students, this life is a golden opportunity to build a solid foundation for future life. It is the time for character building. This is an important time to strengthen your knowledge. At this time, curiosities begin to develop. Knowledge becomes intense. The child gets ready to learn by taking admission in the school. The scope of his knowledge expands. He gets attached to text-books. He starts tasting the knowledge which keeps nurturing him for a lifetime.

When a student who wants to earn knowledge becomes humble, then his path becomes easier. When he approaches the teacher with humility and reverence, the teacher happily blesses him a with a learning experience. He teaches him ethics and social norms, solve problems of mathematics, and develop a scientific attitude in him. He is taught language so that he can express his ideas. In this way, student life becomes progressive achieving success and perfection.

Student life is a period for embracing human qualities. For the attainment of learning, one has to suffer a lot. Without being heated in the fire, gold does not become pure. Therefore, the ideal student only wants to learn without seeking happiness in life. He bears the qualities of patience, courage, honesty, perseverance, devotion towards teacher, self-respect, and continues on the path of life. He lives a moderate life so that there is no hindrance in learning. Knowledge is not contained only in books. The words of knowledge do not come only from the of teachers. Knowledge flows like a stream. Student life is the time to drink from this flowing water. Be it the playground or having a conversation, an opportunity to travel or the laboratory of the school, knowledge is everywhere. Student life is a period of assimilating the knowledge scattered in these different forms. Health related things are learnt in this phase. The body is strengthened through exercise and sports during this period of life. Apart from studying during student life, a student learns life skills that contribute to growth of a wholesome person.

The merit-demerit, good-bad, virtue-sin, and religion-agnosticism are everywhere. They have to be identified during the student life itself. The smart student absorbs the essence and gives up the useless stuff. Learning and virtue are essence and vice is transitory. During student life, a certain distance should be maintained from vices. Good habits should be adopted. One should learn to respect the elderly. The importance of speaking in a nice manner should be understood. One should stay avoid intoxicants. Special attention should be paid to physical and mental hygiene. Environmental improvement programmes should be actively participated in.

Achieving goals requires hard work, perseverance and unwavering confidence. Good and bad friends are found during student life. Seeking the company of good friends, you should always move forward towards your goal. The foundation of student life rests on discipline. Therefore, every student should adopt discipline in life. Discipline motivates man to move forward in life and protects him from vices. The hard work in the beginning makes life successful.

Student and Stress

Today, along with the rising standards of living, materialistic competition is also at its peak, the side effects of which are seen in the form of a stressful lifestyle. It is quite sad that today the tendency of students to learn with diligence and hard work is disappearing. They want to take shortcuts in every sphere of life. Parents also put unnecessary pressure on children for study and career. They do not want to understand that the intellectual ability of each child is different due to which every student cannot come first in the class.

From childhood, children should be taught that failure is the biggest key to success so that if the child fails due to any reason, he is not stressed by the fear of family and social disgrace.

The pressure of exams, the fear of humiliation by classmates, the teachers scolding the child and their inability to tolerate sarcasm often push students towards this path of stress. In the fast paved life of the city, children are maturing ahead of time. As a result, they want to make their own decisions. They end up taking wrong decisions many times if they do not get the expected results according to the decisions they have taken. Children are not machines or robots. They should be taught good values from childhood so that they choose their own destination but do not lose confidence. If you want children to be tolerant, patient, fearless, serene, stable, then change yourself first.

Today's education makes children a doctor, engineer or officer, but whether he becomes a good, upright human being depends on his values. A bird needs two wings to fly high. Similarly, human beings also need both types of education to achieve the higher goal of life. Worldly education will help him earn his livelihood and moral education make his lifc valuable.

The Challenge of Examination

The changing nature of the current education and the burden of the curriculum has entangled students of all ages in a spate of problems. To achieve the goal in student life, it is really necessary to be focused on three things – positive thinking, commitment to hard work and the ultimate determination.

Student life is a period when your future is determined. The goal of making the blurred picture of our golden future clear has to be set during the student life itself. Staying away from addictions, focusing on books and associating with people who can give right direction to unsure steps with high thinking – these should be considered as the main stages of cultivation in student life.

Examination time is the most stressful time for the students. The fear of examination just keeps haunting them. During this important time, children should be fit and positive. To overcome the fear of examination, first of all, it is necessary to instil confidence in oneself. Self-confidence is a psychological weapon that can dispel all kinds of anxiety and nervousness within minutes. Go to the examination hall with full confidence at the time of examination. Having a positive attitude towards writing answers to questions can present a beautiful view only by wearing an attire of confidence. In order to have an enduring sense of confidence, it would be better to inculcate the habit of memorizing the answers and writing them down again and again. By writing repeatedly, hands and pen also move in the direction that the student categorically needs.

In order to put an end to the fear of examination and get good marks, students should keep some important things in their mind -

- At the time of examination, it is important to pay attention to time management. Studying by dividing your daily routine according to the various subjects of the examination should be considered a scientific method.
- In order to maintain the correctness of spelling in subjects like Hindi, English and Sanskrit, it may be appropriate to write again and again.
- At the time of examination, after you receive the question paper, first start writing the answers to the questions about which you are more confident.
- Do not consider any type of examination or question paper as a burden and study in a normally relaxed environment.
- Make a habit of studying from the beginning of the year so that the burden of studying the entire syllabus at the time of examination can be avoided and the benefit of continuous learning can also be gained.
- Subjects like Mathematics, Physics and Accounts should be prepared as group studies so that each other's doubts can be solved easily.
- Instead of memorizing the questions and answers of any subject, read them again and again and prepare for the exam by preparing some points by writing them down in your own words.

Life and Difficulties

According to Chanakya, one has to face adversity in life directly or indirectly. There can be two ways of coping with the difficult situations in life. Either we run away from them or try to overcome them. There is no place anywhere in this world for those who are afraid of life and run away. When one challenge is complete, we have to be ready to face another one. The real victory of our life comes when we do not lose our mental balance even in the most troubled times. Our life is like that of a ship which has to face the sea's raging currents, adverse winds and whale and sharks every moment. There is no such challenge in front of a ship that is standing in the port. If the ship is ready, then it is its duty to face the challenges by going into the sea. In the same way, the man is created to accept challenges.

When there are obstacles in life, we should awaken the inner forces and experience new type of energy. It should not be forgotten that the life of a human being is meant to face struggles as well as to love and cooperate. The real goal of life should be to help oneself as well as help others. It should not be forgotten that a man alone cannot do anything. The identity of any human being is also connected with another human being. It also does not mean that we become dependent on others. It is seen that often we are unhappy because we have great expectations from others. When these expectations are not met, we feel sad.

Actually, in life we should develop a sense of gratitude. We should be indebted to all beings of the world who have played their role in our development and nourishment in one form or the other. It should not be forgotten that there is no problem that cannot be solved. It is morning after every night.

Why do we stay unhappy? Because instead of positive thoughts, negative thoughts dominate us. Whenever we think, we think negatively. No human can ever lead a happy life with such thoughts. Life should be like a yogi – occupied with oneself, one who gives importance to karma. Along with karma and religion, spirituality should also be important in life. Along with the physical progress of man, spiritual progress is also necessary. The life of a spiritually developed conscious person is different. The simple events of life do not make him unhappy. He feels that the whole world is his. He considers everyone living in it as his own. He forgets that he was born alone and has to die alone.

Struggle is the Ladder to Success

Set goals and work hard and the you will reach the destination certainly. Instead of being discouraged by failure, face it as a challenge. Former US President Abraham Lincoln suffered failure for 28 consecutive years. But he did not lose courage and managed to become president because of the struggle. Narendra Modi, who belonged to the poor section, reached the post of Prime Minister of the country after running a tea shop. Students should aim for success by treating them as their role models.

If the cornerstone is firm then the building built on it is also durable and permanent. Similarly, if the student has spent his life in hard work, discipline, restraint and regulation, then his future life will surely be pleasant, beautiful and beneficial for the family, society and country. Sleeping on time, getting up on time, studying on time, exercising on time, eating on time, sitting in the company of scholars, staying away from contaminated thoughts and misconceptions are the hallmarks of a smart student.

In fact, student life is the time to get trained for facing difficulties in the future life. Perhaps with the same background, Abraham Lincoln wrote in a letter to his son's teacher – "It is possible to truly enjoy victory only by learning to lose".

It is a time to learn the methods to solve future problems. The personal, social and moral behaviour of the student plays a very important role in the life of a society or a nation. The student's virtuous and sober behaviour, obedience, modesty and humility, sensitivity, ability to adapt himself to the situation makes him dear to teachers, seniors and to the society.

The Effect of Conduct

Whether our intention is to harm anyone or not, we should not behave under the influence of anger or greed or selfishness. The first premise of morality is that we should avoid destructive behaviour. When we talk of morality, we mean that we should be disciplined. And being disciplined means that we have control over our lives and we are not under the influence of laziness or other disturbing mental conditions that prevent us from achieving our life's goals.

Thus, good moral conduct actually means to engage in creative work. Getting a good education while studying hard is an example of this. This requires strict discipline – self-discipline to study, to learn. But if we want to achieve something positive in our life, then we must acquire qualifications for that, we must practice and that requires discipline.

Ways to Become a Smart Student

- We are taught to be disciplined since childhood, whether at home or at school. Students who follow discipline in the true sense are truly smart students.
- Having positive thinking is important for every person, and when we talk about a smart student, it is necessary for such a student to have positive thinking. Thinking positively and staying positive keeps us away from many kinds of stresses and troubles.
- As a smart student, you always have to be alert towards your studies. Nothing is more important for you than your studies. Study alone can make you a successful person in the future.
- Always learn something good and keep doing something new. Your intelligence is sharpened by learning something good and new. For this, you can read good books, learn new languages. You can learn everything that can make you a smart student.
- Be a good person and always help people. It is said that we get back what we give. When you help someone today, maybe they will also help you tomorrow. Therefore, a smart

student is also a good aide. Your helpful nature can also make you a successful person.

- Do not harm anyone. The evil person loses credibility in the eyes of others. Smart people never cause harm to anyone. Instead, they seek goodness in people.
- Never hurt anyone. Smart people always give happiness rather than hurting people. The one who hurts people is neither smart nor truly successful.
- It is good to have a habit of asking questions. But it is not necessary to ask questions about everything. Find the answers to what you think is important to you.
- Instead of "I", give more importance to "you". By doing this, the person in front will be influenced by your behaviour and will also respect you.
- Help the needy. If you see only your benefit, then you will never be able to achieve far-reaching goals.
- To become a smart student, it is important that you have a big goal for your studies. Today, most of the students go to school but do not set any goals for their studies. In this way, they are caught off-guard when the examination approaches. Then during examinations, they start studying as if they are participating in a marathon.
- The student who understands the purpose of his studies always tops his studies. Therefore, set a big goal for your studies and be a smart student.

Swami Vivekananda says, "From childhood, one should live in the company of an ascetic with a bright character so that you will always have living ideal of the highest knowledge in front of you. Lying is a sin, there is no benefit in just learning by rote. One must take a vow to observe complete celibacy during the student life; only then will reverence and devotion rise in the heart. Otherwise, why would one who does not have devotion and piety not tell lies?"

Acharya Chanakya says that knowledge, valour, wisdom, courage, strength and patience are our true friends who help us in our moments of difficulties. They are our real benefactors during bad times. The person who lives through them will surely succeed. Only those who have achieved success by confronting many challenges can enjoy its fruits. In the face of challenges, an indescribable power arises within us, which helps us overcome all the obstacles coming in the way. There is no royal road to success in life. Read the life-story of any successful person; you will find that he has found his destination only after overcoming many difficulties.

❑

Student Life and Discipline

"A lazy person or student has neither present nor future."

–Chanakya

The biggest discipline during student life is the proper use of time and the biggest obstacle in it is sleep. In today's era, the biggest problem that the students face is sleep. The best rule or discipline of student life is considered to be sleeping early at night, waking up early in the morning and studying. There are two situations with the student - one of principles and the other of behaviour. Every student follows the principles and when practical life starts, then he faces the test as to what did he learn? Life does not always run according to the principles. On most occasions, life follows practicality.

According to Acharya Chanakya, student life is the period of embracing human qualities. For attaining knowledge, one has to suffer a lot. Without burning in fire, gold does not become pure. Therefore, the ideal student only focusses on learning and not pleasure in life. He adopts the qualities of patience, courage, honesty, perseverance, devotion to guru, and self-respect, and continues on the path of life. He lives a moderate life so that there is no hindrance in the process of learning. Knowledge is not present only in books. The words of knowledge do not come only from the master. Knowledge flows like a stream. Student life is the time to drink from this stream. Be it the playground or the time of discussion, an opportunity to travel or the laboratory of the school, knowledge is present everywhere. Student life is a period for assimilating the knowledge scattered in these different forms. Health related things are learnt during this phase of life. The body is strengthened through exercise and sports during this phase. In addition to studies, another skill could be learnt that can be used when required.

When you step out in the world after your student life, sometimes you will feel that you were better off in the classroom. Eating and drinking, reading, playing and sleeping - apart from this, there was no hassle, no responsibility, no stress. While studying, you wonder when it will be complete and you will be able to leave home and see the outside world and enjoy it. But this world is not as easy as you think. There are many types of challenges and conflicts in it. Study a lot, work hard, struggle hard, earn a lot of money, name and fame.

Believe in Mind

There can be no courage without faith and assurance and half the battle lies in the belief that we can do what we want. There is power in faith through which light can be brought to the desolate world. Faith can turn a stone into a God, and lack of belief can make the man created by God stone hearted. Faith is life and doubt is death. They won because they believed that they would win.

The student should not get caught in deception, fraud, confusion and should concentrate and walk on his path of duty. A person's heart, mind is very fickle and can misguide a student in a short span of time. It can disturb his mind. The mind should be kept under our control so that it does not wander nor the student wanders according to it. The student's mind acts like a motor vehicle. The more speed it gets, the more it pulls or goes in the direction that it wants to go. Now it is up to a person's mind and intellect how much speed it wants to give.

By being constantly aware of personality development, students can leave a golden mark of their supremacy on the horizon of success and achievements. The superior personality will be good for you, your family and those around you. You will make your valuable contribution in building a better, beautiful and civilized society. The world will be heaven in many ways – full of superior and capable human beings.

Strength and Ability

The basis of power is organized effort or energy. Energy cannot be organized without putting the body and mind to work at one task at a time. When an ordinary magnifying lens is used for focusing sun rays on a board, the rays of the sun make a hole in it in a few minutes. At the same time, if the rays are not concentrated, the board will not even become hot in the slightest. Human mind is also very much like a magnifying lens because just as the lens focuses the sun's rays in one place, the brain also collects its inner elements and motivates them to do some work in sync. Misuse of power is the problem and harnessing power is the solution. The problem is the misuse of youth power or the possibility of misusc, and the use of this power is the solution to the problem. Youth power can be put to good use by training in self-control, discipline, celibacy.

Power arises from systematic knowledge. But remember that through its use, it develops from within. One can become a moving compendium of knowledge even without having any power. This knowledge becomes power only to the extent that it is organized, classified and put to work. Some of the best educated people have less common sense than those who are called fools. But the difference between these two is that the first one used whatever knowledge they had while the other one did not.

Power can be achieved through organized and cooperative efforts! Dozens of fully trained soldiers, owing to their united strength, control the crowd of thousands, which is rudderless and disorganized. Periodic relaxation is required to keep gaining strength. Strength, energy, and motivation are essential. In the absence of these, we will not be able to do justice to fulfilling our responsibilities and obligations. Whoever you are, wherever you are, whatever your scope of work, whether you have unlimited responsibilities or obligations or troubles, if you manage the time properly, then many of your difficult tasks will also be simplified, the stalled work will be completed. Your confidence will increase, you will get appreciation, respect and praise, and you will experience satisfaction and happiness yourself. By staying busy, your health will be fine, you will feel hungry, sleep will be good, you will be happy, refreshed and cheerful. There will be a dignified glow on the face, mind will be relaxed. By dividing time, you will be able to do more work in a short time.

Doubt and Uncertainty

Doubt and uncertainty are two conflicting directions. Where there is doubt, you cannot reach a decision. If a person has a doubt that he does not know whether he will be able to do this work or not, he can never achieve success. To be successful, determination is required. As long as you do not remove bad luck, impossible and indecision, doubt, etc. from your dictionary, you cannot get success in any area of life. If you have such beliefs, then one day it will be impossible for you to even stand on your feet. Open your eyes and understand the truth that you have to do something and become something in life.

Doubt and uncertainty block your path to success. This gives rise to a kind of indirect anxiety in your mind. As a result, your unconscious mind is unable to take the requisite command to do that particular task. When you perform a task half-heartedly, it is never successful. Practically, the person in front of whom your work is presented, measures your eligibility within the same boundary line. You should keep in mind that there is never any scope for excuses between life and the challenges of the work field.

Doubt is not a bubble of water which dissolves in an instant. Doubt is a comet which extends from one end to the other in the sky. Do you know what a comet symbolizes? Fear, dread, danger. Doubt is your enemy. It instils fear in your heart, due to which you accept defeat in the task you had full confidence of winning.

Doubt weakens your anti-crisis power. Doubt also serves to weaken your confidence and the thought that is required to do the work successfully. As long as the mind is disturbed, it can never think effectively. It cannot give birth to any creative thought or action. Doubt also naturally makes our process of contemplation and meditation sluggish and also reduces our power. Its abandonment is inevitable.

Truth

Truth is a quality that manages your time and you are successful in doing more useful and profitable tasks in less time. Being able to face the truth is the biggest sign of your emotional and mental strength. If you are going to overcome an obstacle then you need to be able to face it. Lying to yourself about what is going on in your business will only hurt you in the end. To accept the truth, keep your eyes, ears, heart and mind alert and only after reaching the right decision, uncover the truth.

Acharya Chanakya says that true character also touches the elemental part of human nature, the soul or the heart. Therefore, one should not make a mistake about personality formation only by learning a showy etiquette. The true character of a man enables him to follow the highest morality even in his day-to-day life.

Real hard work is the key to success. Any goal can be achieved with true dedication and hard work. There may be a delay in achieving the goal, but no one can stop success. By attaining true education, we achieve a new life, hypnotized state. And we learn a new lesson about life from the point of view of that new life. This world appears as if a new light had emerged in front of our eyes. It is only with such education that we can build the foundation of life, welfare of society and nation. The foundation of fraternity can be attained only as a result of this education.

A feeling of true bliss is associated with the conscience. There is no limit to the enthusiasm and optimism born of this feeling. Between a true student and an impostor, there is a difference of principles, not of methodology and style. The true student is the one who faces difficulties with joy and with that experience, produces success from his or her designated path for the future. None of the paths in the world have been laden with carpets. Each route has thorns, boulders, pits and numerous traps. Success is achieved by crossing them. Remember, the fate of only those people changes who want to change it.

Truth is the pinnacle of greatness of personality. It is put to use by justice. The values of truth, non-violence, love and renunciation were the same five thousand years ago, they are the same today and will be the same after five thousand years to come. Since the principles keep changing, the thing which seems wrong today may seem right after 20 years and maybe what is right now would seem wrong after 20 years. Therefore, while planning life, do not just think of today. Plan ahead keeping the situation 20 years ahead in mind. Time is changing very fast. If you do not understand its value or do not catch it, then you will miss it.

The effect of truth distinguishes one man from others. Just as Dharmaraja Yudhishthira's chariot used to rise above the earth due to truthful speech, that is, it was the most different, in the same way truthful speech separates one man from others, that is, he joins the category of successful people. On the contrary, falsehood causes distance between people, that is, it makes them join the category of failures. Speaking untruth for trivial matters only suits those who choose to fail. Not exercising our abilities faithfully is just like standing with our hands tied while knowing everything.

Alertness

Alertness is a kind of awareness that keeps your mind and brain awake. All the tasks of the student who is awake are managed. Being unaware also means how conscious you are while organizing your work and your time. When you do some work consciously, then there is very little scope for making a mistake. Not only this, the conscious student never wastes time. Just as the conscious student understands the value of his time, he also knows the value of the other students' time. If you live your life in such awakened state that all the obstacles in your path are clearly visible then you will surely succeed.

There is a huge difference between alertness and self-observation of self-expanding growth. Self-observation leads to frustration, to widespread duality, while alertness is a process of freedom from self-action. Awareness means being alert to your daily activities, to your thoughts, to your actions and to others, to watch that other carefully. You can do this only when you love someone, when you have a deep interest in something. When I want to know myself, my whole personality, the whole content and not just one or two layers, it is clear that there should be no room for tendency to criticize.

Alertness is freedom. It brings freedom, it provides freedom. On the other hand, self-observation is about duality, that is the process of being closed within the realm of self so that frustration and fear will always remain. Self-observation leads to more frustration because the desire for change remains hidden and the change is only a modified continuation. Alertness is a condition in which there is neither condemnation nor justification of support. Students have to overcome all these challenges.

❑

13

Road to Success

"Education is a friend during travel, wife is a friend at home, medicine is friend for patient and after death, religion is a friend."

–Chanakya

Acharya Chanakya says that student life is as tough as asceticism. If you want to get good results, then it has to be taken as austerity. There are two situations in front of the student – one is principles and the other is behaviour. Every student follows the principle and when practicality starts in life, then it is a test of what he learnt? Life does not always function according to the principles. On most occasions, it works according to practicality.

India is second to none in the field of technology. We have also done almost everything that the world is doing. We extracted oil and gases from the sea. We extracted everything from the womb of the earth for which the world is known. We have also reached the last layer of the sky from where information and technology is doing its work. We have left no stone unturned in the field of health and science either. We have done a lot and we are also proud of it.

But even after all this, most young people of India look for an opportunity to go to a foreign country. They believe that there are more good opportunities abroad for building careers than there are in India. There may be partial truth in this matter, but that does not mean that there is no possibility of opportunities in India. One day, India will achieve whatever the developed countries have, but no country will be able to match the valuable wealth that we have in form of our culture.

If you are fond of studying abroad and earning foreign exchange, then definitely do it; there is no harm in that. But never forget your culture and the potential of India. This land has a lot of glory, a lot of possibilities, a lot of life. No matter how far and high you reach, always maintain your sense of being Indian.

Considering the outside world and the challenges out there, the mind, brain and vision of the students are immature. Therefore, the student needs the support of the guru. In the event of losing the path, only the guru shows the right path. Remember one thing that a guru does not mean that you receive diksha from someone and that he will be your guru. Teachers are definitely your gurus. But apart from them, parents, other elders of the family, your seniors etc. can also be your teachers. Arrogance is a big obstacle in the way of connecting with the guru. Until your ego melts away, the mind-brain will not understand the need of the guru. Eliminate the ego and learn whatever good in life you can from those whose experience will be useful and adopt from those whose explanation would show the right path. Opportunities and experiences do not come back once they leave. So, take advantage of every good opportunity in the right way.

Religion, Artha, Kama and Moksha

Indian culture is incredible, and in some cases, it is very vast. There are four words in it, which if understood and implemented in life, it becomes meaningful. Today these words may be new and weighty for you, but when you practise them in life, you will find how remarkable their meaning is. These words are – Dharma, Artha, Kama and Moksha. Collectively, they have been called Purushartha in Indian culture. Whatever you become – politician, doctor, engineer, businessman, housewife – whatever it is – but one who understands the meaning of these four words, his life management will be perfect. All the management of life revolves around these four words.

If the question is asked correctly, the answer will also be correct. So, do not find faults in things, rather ask for suggestions to make them better. Then life will be joyful.

The best rule or discipline during student life is considered to be sleeping early at night and getting up early in the morning to study. Our sages and saints have said that the person who gets up early in the morning and studies and who sees the rising sun, his memory, his learning power, analysing capacity, concentration will expand so much that even bad luck cannot stop him from rising high. He himself is eligible to create his own destiny.

Nowadays, many children get up at eight or nine o'clock and looking at the sun, they think that it rises in the same big size. They do not know that the sun rises in the form of a beautiful, red-coloured sphere.

The point is that sleep is a big obstacle in getting up early in the morning and studying. If sleep is not controlled, then it will be difficult to reach a high position in life. Remember, whoever has instilled a habit of getting up early in the morning has gained a lot.

However, it is very difficult to get up early beating the early morning sleep. The sleep at that time is such that the man becomes helpless before it. While sleeping at night, he resolves that he will wake up early in the morning. But he forgets his own resolve in front of that sweet morning sleep. There are many people who even get into a fight with family members if they try to wake them early.

If you achieve any success in life, remember that it is not yours alone. Many people contribute directly or indirectly to it. Teachers, parents, siblings, friends, life-partner - all lend their support in one way or the other. Someone gives you encouragement, someone gives guidance, someone gives time, someone makes sacrifices. Only then can you become a successful person. Be thankful to them, thank them.

No one gets anything in the world without hard work. God also blesses one who asks for anything in return of labour. Therefore, no matter how famous you become and start to live in the modern world never stop working.

Achieve Your Aim

Chanakya has said that we should develop the art of utilizing whatever power and strength God has given us. Our talent develops naturally when we are ready to do certain tasks in a definite and determined manner.

On the battlefield, the commander who sets his goal beforehand wins. No matter how large the army is, it is impossible to conquer the enemy by just moving it around and hitting the enemy at various places.

Behind all the battles that Napoleon Bonaparte won in his life, his concentration and focus on goal were at play. To achieve success, a person must give focus all his powers to fulfil that resolution. In our life, we see a variety of attractive and enticing actions and behaviours. Many times, our mind gets so attracted to them that sometimes we keep shifting our focus from one task to another. The result is that the main target gets lost.

After setting a goal, we can wholeheartedly work towards fulfilling it only when we divert attention from other temptations. A person who makes a task his life's mission achieves complete victory.

Nowadays, in many countries around the world, practical training is being given more importance than theoretical courses. In our country too, radical changes are taking place in the structure of education. The only purpose behind all these changes is how we can use the talents of human beings for specific purposes. Not only this, the aim of many training courses is also to acquire the power of theoretical concentration. Till now, the kind of education that is imparted in schools is based on the principle that a person can learn to write, speak, calculate and think purely. But modern educationists have recognized the importance of giving such education to children that they can decide the path of livelihood in future.

There are two types of things that come to mind when focusing on the principle of definite purpose and projecting a departure towards your goal – one is that a person has been doing some work for a long time with all the effort and diligence even if there have been difficulties. If he does not achieve the expected success compared to other, should he take up some other work? Or should he always be engaged in the same work? If, after years of experience of failure of the same work, we get to know the real reason and we come to conclusion that this reason is so strong that we cannot remove it, then it is appropriate to take up another work. But leaving one task and hastening to the other soon does not yield the expected results.

Understand the Constraints

The obstacles we face in our life and work strengthen us. It is well known that gold becomes pure only after bearing the fiery flames of fire. Mahatma Gandhi used to say that there are some wars in which defeat is victory. Man also needs to make repeated efforts and wait patiently. Because it has also been seen many times that when we are close to reaching the precious pearls hidden at the bottom of the sea, we are exhausted and we go back to the shore. If we had stayed on for a while, we would surely have succeeded. Another important thing to keep in mind is that every precious thing found in life must be worth its price.

If the willpower is strong and the skill of dreaming becomes a hobby of a person, then the goals themselves carve a path. To overcome the obstacles, we have to create a greater system. We should not think that we will achieve success only with the help of a strong will. Strong willpower is the key to success, but we must also have the skill to clean that key, put it in the lock and rotate it.

We can reach our real destination only by removing the obstacles on the way. Knowledge and prudence are absolutely necessary to make the adversity favourable. If there are thorns in the path, then the conscience says that remove them, burn them or bury them in the ground. What is the use of shedding blood in vain by walking on those thorns? Unless adversity is removed, favourable situation cannot take its place. Unless favourable circumstances are produced, the path cannot be proceeded upon. And adversity can be transformed into favourable situation only when the actions we perform are full of wisdom and knowledge. The goal cannot be achieved by running with our eyes blindfolded. With the light of wisdom and knowledge, golden lamps of achievements can be lit even on the dark path. When we venture with prudence and knowledge, the mountain standing on the path can also be removed, or a road can be built over it. But there is no use of banging your head on the mountain where the path cannot be built.

The real education of man does not take place in school and college; it takes place in the midst of sufferings and deprivations. One who tries and conquers difficulties gets success. If there were no difficulties, there would not be success either. In the absence of struggle, there would be no victory. The progress of man lies in the effort that he makes to achieve success or victory. The more adversities a person faces to achieve success, the more important is his success.

Overcome Doubt

Doubt and scepticism are obstacles in our path of success. When our mind is divided into two parts, then our power also gets divided in two different directions. It can also be understood in a way that the more we divide our work in different parts, the results achieved also comes in that many parts.

It is natural for a human being that if a small doubt arises in his mind about a task, then even the simplest events also support that doubt. There is also a time when the excess of doubt affects our intelligence in a negative way. In other words, doubt is the originator of despair.

Whatever are the characteristics of our personality, we should use them openly. Anything that we do not use gradually disappears.

Psychologists say that what we think and do throughout the day is uninterruptedly shaping our future. In fact, true achievement is neither in collection nor in attainment, but in creativity. Creativity can never take place with scepticism.

Positive Thinking

Chanakya says that God resides where there are auspicious thoughts. What is God? The divine powers in the human body are gods. Both gods and demons reside in the mind of the man. The soul sees and knows both these elements. Our situation is a result of our thoughts.

Our thoughts have a very strong impact on our lives. Before doing any work, its idea is born first and then our efforts in that direction begin. The kind of thoughts and the same kind of efforts result in similar results. Positive thoughts increase the energy of our life by leaps and bounds. All the people who have been successful in this world were all positive thinking people. Our thinking takes the form of truth and faces us. It is said that a man's face is a mirror of his thoughts. Whatever and whichever way we think, it gradually gets engraved on our face.

You cannot develop real talent without getting rid of the tricks to find success through despair and shortcuts. Always welcome thoughts full of hope and faith. Within a few days, you will be surprised that the posts, the chairs which you have long desired to occupy are attracted towards you. The full container cannot be filled further. It is also important to note that those who want to fill the lives of others with achievements need the art of complying sympathetically.

Face Challenges

The weakness of all of us is that we are less interested in playing and are more interested in losing and winning. We do not want to play with all our might and dream that someone can put the victory in our lap safely. There are many people who do not make their mistakes exciting. We should think over ourselves, our efforts. We should accept our strengths and flaws without any hesitation.

Hang on

It is the duty of God to make the person who has the ability to stay firm in difficult times successful. In fact, staying firm is that art of living life which opens the doors of success for us. Those who search steadily can find anything.

The journey to success is associated with gradual and steady development. Everyone knows that the beginning of any major journey starts with the first step. Those who have progressed towards the realization of their dreams know that even small achievements in the early days worked for them as a great source of energy.

What really happens is that our small successes come together and become a cause for a big success for us. It can also be said that by adding successes, we create a bridge on which the chariot of our progress runs again without stopping.

Soon after starting the task, we start going from one thing to another. The scope of our contact with people keeps on expanding. We start to know about the things that we were unaware of till yesterday. At the same time, we also get to know about such opportunities which help us to discover our real talent. We are naturally filled with so much confidence and energy that we fulfil those dreams and desires about which millions of people in the world just keep thinking.

Remember that we get most of the opportunities by chance. But such coincidences are available only to those who know the art of converting those coincidences into success. Only those who stand patiently with their net spread in the sea get fish. Such occasions are not available to those people who sit in the house with doors closed and only day dream.

There is a quality inside each person which distinguishes him from everyone else. Talented people develop that quality so much that it becomes an introduction to their personality.

Chanakya says that proper education, practical knowledge of the subject, positive thinking, etc. are the qualities on the strength of which we can increase the sharpness of our brain. Remember, our intelligence becomes the cause of real success by salvaging us from many crises. Not only mental but also physical exercise is very important for the efficiency and attentiveness of the brain. According to a research, people who exercise regularly get better marks in mental tests. This is because the brain also has muscles. When you do physical exercise, the blood circulation of the brain increases and its ability to work and the ability to understand subjects also increases.

Success is about achieving the goals chosen by a person – goals that a person aspires to and works for, regardless of what they are. This is a positive result of our efforts. When the chain of achievements is put together and associated with the great achievements of life, it is known as success. Success has different meanings for each person. Success has many forms and definitions. It all depends on what you are looking for in life. Success is a journey, not a destination; You have to keep moving forward.

The meaning of success varies from person to person. Success does not come to you, you go to it. Success is subject to interpretation based on the individual's education, past experiences, roles, personal motivations and goals. Carefully analyse your definition of your success based on your beliefs. When you achieve success, many times it is it is worth evaluating and many times it is not. Very few people get success by chance.

Confidence Encourages You

According to Chanakya, self-confidence is the first and essential condition for achieving success in life. You have to build the courage to look within yourself and to believe in yourself. Then there is no power that can distract you from your goal.

Eminent writer Swett Marden used to say that self-reliance and confidence have always been more effective than friendship, lineage, recommendation and money. Confidence is the best capital in the world. This removes most obstacles and helps overcomes most difficulties. There are many acts of great courage accomplished by self-confidence as compared to any other human virtue.

Firm intention makes the biggest task smaller. Self-confidence is faith in itself. Whenever we repeat in our mind the resolve that 'I will do this thing,' then you can definitely believe that half the work is already completed. Confidence is the basis of the strength to stay on your path even during the strong storm of obstacles. It is universally accepted that there is no problem that cannot be solved. Obstacles also bring with it signs of resolution.

For confident people who are constantly moving forward on their path of progress, streams of help flow from unheard and unintended sources. There is no need to get frustrated if you have to stop or retreat for a while due to unexpected interruptions.

Self-confidence is a light that shows us the right path even in the darkest of times. Success is attained only by self-confidence and success is supplemented by self-confidence. Whenever we start a task, we cannot guarantee complete success in it. Yes, if we do not leave the path of confidence till the work is completed, then the chances of success definitely increase. It is also important to know here that only success increases confidence. The pleasant feeling of success in our work and efforts boosts our confidence. Financial independence, self-reliance, good health, beauty, material comforts, achievements, peaceful life are the elements that give wings to our confidence. Many people who face the truth of life and those who have a passion for tackling difficulty are also found to be rich in self-confidence. There is also a lot of confidence in upright, true and good people.

Two types of factors play an important role in boosting our confidence – earned factors and unearned factors. Factors that are earned include education, professional achievements, diet, success achieved in a job or business, development of a particular quality, hobby or talent, while unearned factors include family status, physical beauty, social environment, caste, religion, gender, sect, etc. Often the conditions that can be acquired are considered more important for the growth of confidence. It also seems appropriate that from a social and constitutional point of view we are also eligible for it.

Many psychologists believe that both earned and unearned factors play an important role in personality building and confidence building. Even though we give more social importance to the earned factors these two factors are not completely different.

By earning a good personality, we can overcome the lack of physical beauty. In the same way, even if the family has high status, the momentary mindset works to lessen our confidence. There are two ways for a man to maintain self-confidence – either he can achieve what he wants to achieve or reduce his expectations and aspirations. Self-confidence does not just appear as a mental state, but it is also reflected in a person's external personality.

A person who is full of self-confidence, it is reflected in his speech, behaviour, lifestyle and other activities, too.

The mental abilities and skills of human beings who attain a high state of self-confidence automatically increase. There is a reflection of faith in their decisions whereas the person who lacks self-confidence becomes lost and keeps rolling like a stone that gathers no moss.

The lack of confidence and hopeless state of mind also adversely affect our health and beauty. Many psychological problems also arise from that. Lack of sleep, loss of appetite, lack of focus in any work, irritability and annoyance arises from lack of confidence. The essential element to build confidence is that we should assess our own status. No human is born with more or less confidence at birth. It is our accomplishments, personality and factors affecting our mind, brain and life that work to decrease or increase our energy.

There are also youngsters who do their work and business with enthusiasm and joy. Their determination is unwavering. Continuous effort becomes their second nature. Such young men reach the pinnacle of progress. Analyse great and successful people. The first reason for their becoming great will be confidence and only confidence.

Acharya Chanakya says that you conquer destiny with your thought. If you understand that thought is the only reason in building the fortunes of humans, then you will not have to take a sword in your hand. The results are an outcome of thoughts.

There is a possibility of a plant drying or dying only when the fertility of soil is reduced or weather becomes completely unfavourable or the plant does not get sunlight or water properly. Similarly, when a person's thoughts become burdensome with inaction, the power of action decreases, enthusiasm and ecstasy are reduced, courage and self-confidence are lost, then his personality becomes totally negative and ineffective. If our mindfulness follows the pure and true path, then the wrong thoughts of others will have no effect on us.

Successful, happy, healthy and influential people use positive and energetic thoughts while thinking. Now it has also been proved by medical research that a hormone called endorphin is found more in the brains of people with positive thoughts. Similarly, in the state of peace, a hormone called neuropeptide is produced, due to which we experience natural and mental happiness and peace. Research by Sheldon Cohen, Carnegie Mellon University, proves that immunity is progressively reduced in individuals with negative thoughts. So, make your thoughts and thinking positive and you will conquer the world. People with positive thoughts are more successful, popular and influential than other people in the society. People are eager to help them on their own. Their biggest and most complex tasks are also accomplished with little effort.

It is true that the deeper we dive putting ourselves at risk, the more precious gems we gather. Actually, taking risks is a way of living life. It has also been said that one does not get benefits without taking risks. The greater the risk, the greater the benefit. There is no need to get into the habit of looking for danger or to look for an opportunity to take risks. Opportunities keep coming all the time, everywhere. Risk is a part of every decision.

Therefore, any work should be done with full spirit. We have to give up the habit of getting scared. Only then we will be able to achieve our se goals.

One who does not learn to take risks gets nervous in times of crisis. Cultivate self-confidence by developing the habit of taking risks and make your personality effective. Remember, a task performed with hard work and power has better chances of becoming successful.

It is essential for a human being to have a goal in life. Unless you know where the bus is going, you do not travel in it. Then how can you live your life without setting goals? Setting goals is very important and family, financial, physical, mental, social, spiritual elements are included in this. Family is an important aspect of our life and livelihood. The economic point is the supporting aspect of livelihood. You cannot do any work without a healthy body.

Create the goal after careful scrutiny and always have a clear vision. Always set a big goal and work towards it after planning properly. Daniel H. Burnham's statement in this regard is noticeable – "Do not make small plans. They do not have the magic to fill the heart of human beings with passion. Make big plans, move to the peaks with full hope and start working".

Many people are afraid to ask for another job once they lose a job. Some people are afraid to go to the manager's cabin after being reprimanded for seeking promotions. Women whose children survived drowning never allow children to go near the water or learn swimming. Such people suffering from misfortune and difficulties have the impression that such incidents are unalterable and they are always unhappy. Individuals with this kind of mentality often regret thinking that their life has been ruined, that they should have taken some other route a few years ago and now it is too late. But defeat is not a matter of shame.

There is a saying that it is far better to try and lose than not to try. Actually, no defeat tells us that we lack merit. It says that our efforts were lacking, which we can overcome if we want.

The person who actually plunges in the struggle, whose face is filled with dust and sweat and blood, who fights bravely, who makes repeated mistakes and misses the goal again and again, who enjoys enthusiasm and strives for a proper cause gets the credit. One who knows that if he does well, he will taste the rare success of achievement and if he fails, his defeat will be a sign that instead of sitting idle, he thought it appropriate to fight. His face will not look like those people who know neither defeat nor victory.

Achievement and credit are like green shady trees growing on the natural path of effort and failure. Very few people understand that our bold mistakes become the steps of success. Defeat is not the cause of our failure, but the failure to recognize the learning, advice and experience that is hidden in defeat makes us fail. We should learn to accept the responsibilities associated with our mistakes and achievements.

Self-discipline also plays an important role in skill development. By self-discipline, it means the person has to control his activities, his tendencies, his habits, thoughts and routine. For example, if you want to get up every day but you cannot, then it means that you lack self-discipline. Additionally, if you are not able to get rid of any bad habit despite determining and resolving many times, then it is a sign of lack of self-control.

People who want to be successful in their life should have complete control over their emotions, feelings, sentiments, thoughts and anger. Developing a habit of taking full interest in the environment around you is also a helpful element in personality development. The world is so vast that it is difficult to understand and know everything about it. But as far as possible, we should always be ready to accept good things and best values from our country, time and environment. In order to establish our reputation in the society, it is necessary that we first know ourselves. We should have a good knowledge of our good points and bad points. We should have a clear idea of our strengths and shortcomings. Only then, by turning our imperfections into merits can we be worthy in others' eyes. A great solution for this is that while making our assessment we should see ourselves as we are and not as we want to be.

People with positive ideology have no difficulty in harmonizing the society. This reconciliation can be even better if we are able to overcome the contradictions in our lives. The difference between our words and our actions is also a form of contradiction. There is a need to overcome this.

It is said that the first impression is your last impression. Therefore, we should have proper attire, behaviour etc. so as to have a good effect on the other people. We should constantly increase our general knowledge. When we find ourselves in unique and difficult situations, then instead of running away from them, we should fight them firmly. We should always train ourselves so that we continuously increase our knowledge. There is a hidden talent in all of us and our aim should be to find and uncover it.

Many times, we start evaluating ourselves and doubting our abilities while performing a task. We have to give up this habit because it affects our confidence negatively. So, just work and do not waste time in thinking about it. All these steps increase our confidence. If we look at the life of any successful person, we will find that it is their confidence which is at work behind their success. They do not allow doubt in their mind to work. They only have a strong belief that they have to succeed in this task.

❑